MW01103722

Anselam and the Academy of Self-Realization

By

David C. Jones

Illustrated by

Wesley T. Jones

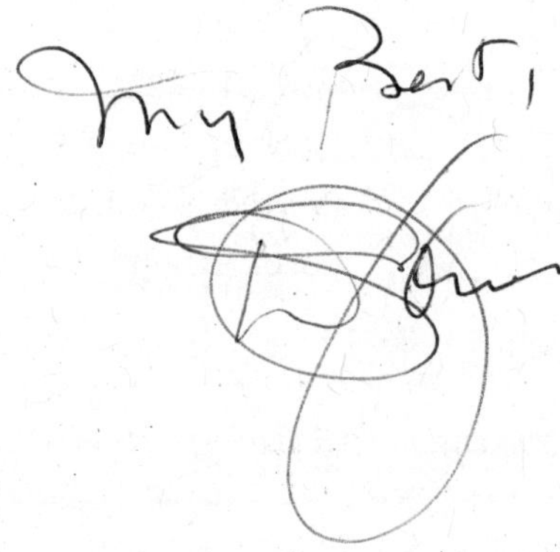

Library and Archives Canada
Cataloguing in Publication

Jones, David C., 1943-
Anselam and the academy of self-realization / David Jones ; illustrated by Wesley T. Jones.

Includes bibliographical references.
ISBN 978-1-55059-374-7

1. Teachers--Psychology.
2. Self-realization.
3. Teaching--Psychological aspects. I. Jones, Wesley T.
II. Title.

LB2840.J67 2009 371.1001'9
C2009-902250-8

We recognize the support of the Government of Canada through the Book Publishing Industry Development Program (BPIDP) for our publishing program.
We also acknowledge the support of the Alberta Foundation for the Arts for our publishing program.

SAN 113-0234
ISBN 978-1-55059-374-7
Printed in Canada
Cover design by Jon Paine

210 · 1220 Kensington Rd NW
Calgary, AB · T2N 3P5
www.temerondetselig.com
p. 403·283·0900
f. 403·283·6947
e. temeron@telusplanet.net

Contents

Prolog

The Embryos

Dear Alma,

A letter after sixteen years!

Strange how one can stop writing after the flurry of epistles we exchanged so long ago, when you and Arn began teaching. But I haven't forgotten you, merely awaited your next message, whenever it came.

So, you now have two children – Larah, fourteen, and young Sanson, five. You taught in a Catholic school for two years until Larah came, stayed home for five years, then taught till Sanson arrived, and you are working again. Their father, Arn, still teaches in a high school, though fatigued, and you serve an elementary school, though troubled. Your marriage is "threatened," your freedom is "quashed," your delight is "dashed," your mood is "growling," and your Spirit "aches for something more." Larah and Sanson feel the disturbance, and the weight saddens them, as one stands at her most vulnerable age, and the other at the start of a new world in school.

A "multiple crisis," you say.

It will pass. Anytime is a good time to turn to all you can be.

The theme of your letter is "embryos" – a word you spat forth several times. Flailing against your profession, you say the school children are embryos, the teachers are embryos, the parents are embryos, the entire school system is an embryo.

Do you know what Rumi, the "whirling dervish," the Sufi, said of an embryo?

Little by little, wean yourself.
This is the gist of what I have to say.

From an embryo whose nourishment comes in the blood,
Move to an infant drinking milk,
To a child on solid food,
To a searcher after wisdom,
To a hunter of more invisible game.

Think how it is to have a conversation with an embryo.
You might say, "The world outside is vast and intricate.
There are wheat fields and mountain passes, and orchards
in bloom.
At night there are millions of galaxies, and in sunlight
the beauty of friends dancing at a wedding."

You ask the embryo why he, or she, stays cooped up
in the dark with eyes closed.

Listen to the answer.

"There is no 'other world.'
I only know what I've experienced.
You must be hallucinating."[1]

Is this not what an embryo thinks? You say your school system does not aim high enough, its summit is too easily scaled, its view is too blinkered, its majesty, too crimped – unaware of its own shortfall, it is like an embryo, yes.

It is fashionable now to know all the questions and none of the answers, as if the answers cannot be found.

Fashionable, too, to think that truth is beyond our ken, that self-realization is a myth. Few laud love, in fact teachers fear the word, and very few know how to instill equanimity.

Sai Baba spoke of a Pundit, a cultured academian, who engaged a boatman to ferry him across the flooded Godavari River: "When the journey over the river started, [the academian] began a lively conversation with the boatman. He asked him whether he had any schooling and when the reply came that he had none, he said sadly, 'Alas! A quarter of your life has gone to waste. It is as if you have drowned those years in the Godavari.' He [then] asked him . . . the time . . . The boatman confessed he did not have a watch nor cared to have one. The Pundit deplored [that] and said, 'Half your life has gone into the Godavari.' His next question was about newspapers; did the boatman read any, what was his favourite paper? The boatman replied that he did not read any nor did he care to know the news. He had enough to worry about already. The Pundit declared forthright that three-quarters of the boatman's life had been liquidated.

"Just then the sky darkened with storm clouds and there was an imminent threat of rain. The boatman turned to the Pundit: it was his turn to put a question. He asked, 'Can you swim?' And when the frightened passenger confessed that he could not, the boatman said, 'In that case, your entire life is now going to merge in the Godavari!' This is the case of the educated in India today. They do not have the training that will help them in distress, or in dire need, to win back their mental poise."[2]

It is the case of the educated in North America, too, and of teachers and pupils in your own school. Real education begins where your modern education leaves off.

But start with your malaise, Alma. Is not your real pain the judgment that you, too, are an embryo and have been one too long? . . . You know, feeling infinitesimally tiny, virtually invisible, daunted by immensity, depressed by incapacity – the stifling discomfort of being a chrysalis too long?

Fondly,

Anselam

Sea of the Self Academy

Dear Alma,

An embryo is not so bad, really, for it always contains its essence. And given the endlessness of our possible expansion, you and I will always be embryos of one sort or another. Maybe this is the difference between us – you see the perplexities of an embryo, but I see the potential. You seek "a completeness, a fulfillment, a fruition, a grandeur presently lacking," and I see that you long to *be* all that you *are*, or put differently, you want to be your Self.

But how?

Perhaps "the Academy" might interest you. "The Sea of the Self Academy," also called "The Academy of the Self."

The Sea of the Self Academy is a school for self-realization. A strange academy, it began millennia ago, with the dawn of consciousness, and begins again with each new moment. Strange too, with no set enrolment, it opens to a single, sincere soul. Unlike other academies that relish complexity, it favors simplicity, and unlike those that contract into tiny specialities, it expands always and all ways, from the workings of subatomic energy to the wonder of universal love. Other schools claim many goals, but the Academy, only one – to awaken the Power and Wisdom of the Self – to create a life of limitless extension beyond the ego, of union with the highest conception and the infinite possibility, a life of beatitude and delight.

Who teaches here? Spirit. To a multitude or one.

How does Spirit teach? Using a million ways or one. There is an equality between teachers and students in this school, and no age limit for either. The student can be a child, and so can the teacher, for a teacher is one who has accepted what she or he is, and that can happen early or late. No fortune or fee is required, merely attention.

Some call The Sea of the Self Academy "The Academy of Self-Realization." Are you interested?

Love,

Anselam

Aala's Gift

Dear Alma and Arn,

So Arn wishes to be included. Good.

Have you ever heard the legend of Aala?

In the beginning, God spoke regularly with his first spirit child, Aala. Now Aala was created already grown, looking probably 17 or 18 years old, as you count time. One day, shortly after her "birth," God said He had a gift for her.

But because Aala did not know what a gift was, her Father said she could ask any number of questions about it.

"I want to give you the greatest gift of all," God began.

"What is it, Father?"

"Here," He handed her a beautiful carved cedar box.

"Is it a box, Father?"

"No, it is *inside* the box," God laughed. "But you may have the box too."

Aala looked carefully at the carving, which she held in two hands, and which looked much like a jewel case made as a small ark, with two smooth ash handles running through the ark and outside on each end, as if the ark could be borne on the shoulders of miniature servants.

As God watched, Aala lifted the ornate cover and peered in. Each side was lined with amethyst crystals, and the bottom was velvet, pinkish mauve, where sat a lustrous, rectangular plate of gold about three inches long and two inches wide.

On the small plate was a single word: "CHOICE."

"How beautiful," said Aala. "But what does it mean?"

"It is a token of my everlasting love for you."

CHOICE

"A choice is?"

"Yes, any choice, but more than that, an infinite number of choices."

"I do not have to make just one choice?"

"No, any number. True love has no limits, no ending. Once born, it expands forever. If I gave you just one choice, you could make a mistake, and if I did not really love you, that mistake could be forever. So you may have as many choices as there are stars in the sky. Then mistakes can become discoveries.

"If I make a choice, will it come true?

"Yes, either immediately or eventually, but you must not make other choices that make your first choice impossible."

"How could I do that?"

"By believing that the first choice is only a dream and that it is not going to happen; or by believing that your weaknesses are stronger than your strengths; or by believing that you do not deserve your first choice. And there are other ways too."

God saw that Aala was confused, and He recognized her confusion as an unsaid question, so without speaking, He suggested a question she might ask.

"Is there a choice more important than the others?" she said timidly.

"Yes, it is the choice of what you want to be, which is really the choice of accepting what you are."

"But who am I?"

"You are an infinite number of things with infinite potential and infinite worth."

"I am?"

"Yes, but you do not have to agree. And you could be unclear about what I am, and therefore what you are.

And even if you are clearer, you will still have the choice of accepting what you are, or not."

Aala was still puzzled.

Then God said, "Why don't you experience things for a time, and as you do, ask me about them, and especially about who you are as you are experiencing them. May I leave you with one small hint?"

"Yes."

"You are like Me."

Thus began the abiding relationship between Aala and God. It is impossible to relate all conversations the two had in the following years, but I wonder if you are interested in the gist of what Aala learned, and of what her descendants taught me?

You see, she was the first Mother, the original Divine Mother, and she founded the Sea of the Self Academy. Many Masters there are in the Academy, but all are sons or daughters of Aala.

Tenderly,

Anselam

P.S. What I call the Masters of the Deep are sons and daughters of Aala, as *humans* see things. They sound like grandchildren of the Father, but the Father has no grandchildren at all, only children.

The Great Heart in the Deep

Dear Alma and Arn,

So you told the story of Aala to your children, and Larah, especially, is intrigued. Good.

You want more about the Academy . . .

Well, start with its name – The *Sea* of the Self Academy – because the vastness of the sea is apt. When I began studies in the Academy ages ago, we were all very anxious to discover the Self and to *live* the discovery, for discovery is nothing without the living. And we soon found that the Self resides in a very deep sea.

In the depths of that sea is a great Heart – a single overlapping reality, a oneness, a closeness, a kinship, a harmony, a love. Living in the embrace of that Heart, which is really their own heart, Masters of Wisdom are also Masters of *Love*; in fact, wisdom without love does not exist. Real love is universal, given to everything, even to things that are not love, that they may *become* love. Masters of the Deep are lovers of this kind. They do not select for their affection this race and not that, this religion and not that, these landscapes, seascapes or life forms, and not those. "Pure love," said Master Krishnamurti, "is like the perfume of the rose, given to all."[3]

If the Heart of Love is the first essence of the deep, what is the first lesson?

Begin with yourself.

"You can spend an eternity looking elsewhere for truth and love, intelligence and goodwill, imploring God and man – all in vain," said Master Nisargadatta Maharaj.

"You must begin with yourself – this is the inexorable law . . . First realize that your world is only a reflection of your self and stop finding fault with the reflection. Attend to yourself, set yourself right – mentally and emotionally . . . Leave alone the reforms and mind the reformer. You talk so much of reforms: economic, social, political. What kind of world can a man create who is stupid, greedy and heartless?"[4]

The Power is in the depths of the ocean of the Self, not somewhere else. So begin there. "Of all the affections the love of oneself comes first," said Maharaj, reversing centuries of instruction to love everyone else first, then, if a crumb be left, flick it to yourself. "Your love of the world is the reflection of your love of yourself, for your world is your own creation . . .[5] Your love of others is the result of self-knowledge, not its cause. Without self-realization, no virtue is genuine. When you realize the depth and fullness of your love of yourself, you know that every living being and the entire universe are included in your affection. But when you look at anything as separate from you, you cannot love it, for you are afraid of it. Alienation causes fear and fear deepens alienation. It is a vicious circle. Only self-realization can break it. Go for it resolutely."[6]

Self-realization requires an intense, unwavering focus, not on others, but on yourself, and it begins with a call from within, and if the call be unheeded, it is repeated aloud by a Master, should a Master be present.

"The guru must act as the alarm clock," said Master Sai Baba; "he should awaken the sleeper to his duty to himself." He is like a mother who teaches her child to speak, but at a certain point the child must speak for himself. "The guru too is like that. He can only repeat, remind, inspire, instruct, persuade, plead; the activity the disciple must initiate. He must jump over the stile himself."[7] He must lift himself from a state of weakness to one of strength. He must stand for himself and assert his inner richness. He must uncover the treasure within, and he must persist.

"To secure pearls," said Baba, "one has to go far out into the sea and dive; simply wading in the shallows and declaring that the pearl story is a myth is a sign of foolishness."[8]

As you dive deep for the pearl that is you, what quality will you need most? What quality is most crucial in seeking self-realization? Humility, receptivity, perseverance, courage, equanimity? Goodness, generosity, or something else?

Intently,

Anselam

To secure pearls one has to go far out into the sea and dive; simply wading in the shallows and declaring that the pearl story is a myth is a sign of foolishness.

Sathya Sai Baba

The Essential Quality

Dear Alma and Arn,

Alma chose love and Arn, courage. Yes, with nothing else these two qualities would carry you to the heights. But more than one Master of the Academy chose differently.

Of all the personal powers or qualities, said the Mother associated with Aurobindo, the key in seeking self-realization was *sincerity*.[9]

Why? I asked myself. Because sincerity is both the flint and the fuel of self-creation, the spark and the sustaining energy. Once initiated, it is a fire, a force, of concentration, and whatever the mind concentrates on strongly enough it creates. Sincerity is powerful because it is pure – it is unalloyed choice, it is unblotted honesty, undiluted by half measures or partial intentions that are always inherently feeble – sincerity is powerful too because in the face of immensity, it is humble, that is, open to suggestion and expansion.

Have you ever tried anything half way? There's no energy in it. Ever been half sincere? There's no force in it.

The human is often a tangle of compromise and false starts, second thoughts and second guesses, where thought, word and deed are sometimes so inconsistent they suggest a tripolar disorder. When thought, word and deed are at odds, sincerity always suffers. When someone says, "a part of me would like that," you know some other part wouldn't, and you also know the other part has diluted the sincerity. You hear, "Well, I'm half inclined . . ." Where is sincerity there?

Sincerity is the guarantee of every virtue, the seal of genuineness. What strange beast would aspiration be without sincerity? How could insincere receptivity exist, or insincere equanimity? What is insincere openness but close-mindedness? Or insincere willingness but unwillingness? Or insincere gratitude but flattery or deceit? How could real courage be insincere? Or true love be insincere, bogus? Insincere attention to one's workers or students, or to Larah and Sanson, is a variation on indifference, carelessness, even callousness. Sincerity makes every virtue genuine.

To realize your highest conception of self, you need to be sincere. You can't say, "Yes, I think I will do that sometime, next month, next year, later, or when the chance comes." If you would become all you can be, as a parent, teacher, or leader, you must, above all else, be sincere, completely focused, completely intent.

That is my explanation for the choice of sincerity.

Interestingly, Alma, you said there was a "beautiful and complete sincerity" in Larah, and an "uncommon and persistent attention" in young Sanson.

Love,

Anselam

Teaching Selfishness or the Majesty of Self

Dear Arn,

"In focusing on the Self so intently," you ask, "are you not teaching selfishness?"

No.

Generally, a selfish person does not value the understanding of the enlightened that they must hurt no one. A selfish person is fearful that what he hoards for himself may be lost. A selfish person sees himself as separate in a world that is constantly separating. Fundamentally, he does not understand that what is good for him is also what is good for others. He is, in short, unwise, and being unwise, he naturally pains himself much. Seeing those whom he purposefully or inadvertently hurts, he is uneasy; taking things before they can or from them, he is anxious; competing and conniving against others, he senses opposition; sharing nothing, he feels guilty – and in these dark moods he is anything but at peace.

If what you have brought yourself is not peace, neither is it love.

So, does such a cur require a self-focus, self-examination, self-expansion, to clarify what he is, to resolve his dilemma? Of course he does, but these self-clarifications and enrichments are anything but conceit or arrogance. If the self is not at peace, you cannot fix it by ignoring it, or by calling your attempt to fix it selfishness.

"You emphasize being as the source of contentment," someone once asked Nisargadatta Maharaj. "Is that not selfish?"

"A most worthy way of being selfish!" exclaimed Master Maharaj. "By all means be selfish by foregoing everything but the Self. When you love the Self and nothing else, you go beyond selfish and unselfish. All distinctions lose their meaning. Love of one and love of all merge together in love, pure and simple, addressed to none, denied to none. Stay in that love, go deeper and deeper into it, investigate yourself and love the investigation and you will solve not only your own problems but also the problems of humanity."[10]

Affectionately,

Anselam

Again

Dear Alma,

"Is this teaching about self-realization, not selfish and egotistic?" you, too, ask.

The answer is crucial because if you are headed toward your highest conception of self and at the same time you believe you are being selfish in doing so, you will compromise your main intent.

No, self-realization is anything but selfish.

Self-realization shapes a loving being whose love extends to *others*, a generous being whose generosity flows to others, a joyful being, whose joy passes to others. It creates a person without the slightest inclination to deceive, defraud or debase. It eliminates impatience, petulance, gracelessness, domination, duplicity, cruelty, chaos, conceit, and judgementalism. How can you be hurt by someone who doesn't demand anything from you, who doesn't want anything from you, who is guided by a wisdom in which no one loses?

How could a person who holds you in reverence be selfish, how could one who is the heart of forgiveness be selfish, how could one who encourages you to love *yourself* be selfish? How could a saint who sees you as one with her ever be negatively self-serving? How could anyone who cheers *your* spiritual expansion, who exhorts *your* success, who rouses *your* self-esteem, who emboldens *your* resolve, who fosters *your* intuition, who spurs *your* imagination, who heals *your* illness ever be considered selfish?

Now substitute "her" for "your" in the above paragraph, and repeat it to Larah – for in doing these things for herself, she will do them for others. And she will not be confused by a religious studies teacher who says, "uplift others, sacrifice yourself; they count, you don't . . . "

Become self-realized, and you also become the perfect example of trustworthiness to your children, and to everyone else. The self-actualized are the most positive souls on the planet, and a single one can neutralize the negativity of tens of thousands.

Love,

Anselam

The Power of the Self-Realized

Dear Alma and Arn,

Yes, there is more Power and Wisdom in the self-realized than you know.

Yogananda once said, "People are often appalled by the power they see expressed in the lives of saints. But remember, you will never find God until you are very strong in yourself. [Because God *is* strength in yourself, I add] Power may exercise less appeal on your mind than other aspects of God, but it is important to realize that divine power, too, is a part of your divine essence."[11]

There is great power in self-realized persons, in Aala's progeny, great focus, great confidence, great love and great peace. Their wisdom has endowed superb clarity. They see the broad panorama of life. With uncommon resolve, they have transcended the mass consciousness with its fixation on cynicism, lack, limitation and loss.

They do not need approval from others.

They have stopped trying to force others into a certain mould.

They feel no need to be right in an argument. They are beyond grudges and resentments, grievances and regrets.

They cannot be offended.

They are remarkably unfettered by dogma and doctrine. Because they have advanced beyond the dogma and seen deeper truths or exceptions to the dogma, they know that dogma is fossilized truth, frozen in time, and because they know there are further revelations, even beyond their present awareness, they never declare a finality to truth.

They are free of dogmas, free of the past. They are not ruled by habits, quirks of personality, or the quibbles of ego.

They have overcome fear, especially the fear of not being good enough.

They have expanded their hearts.

They have broken the embryo's shell, the shell of human consciousness and have entered other worlds where the natural restrictions of human life, even the laws of physics, have dissolved. These laws, as you know them, are just one script in the cosmic drama.

They live where answers come to the most difficult question, any question, where the energies around them are activated and where love is complete.

They are self-possessed, and in this self-possession there is great power.

They control their reality.

They create their own destiny, a destiny of graciousness, goodness, generosity, enthusiasm, beauty and joy. Because they have evolved into pure spirit, they are a vortex of pure positivity. Their personal radiance can instantly transform anyone who enters its orbit, who meets it, and *feels* it. And when you are transformed either by that radiance or by your own, only then can you understand the difference between a mere intellectual recognition of truth and the magnificent totality of knowing that truth within and *living* it.

Blessings,

Anselam

Teachers

Do You Need a Teacher?

Dear Arn,

Do you need a guru, a teacher, to become self-realized, you wonder.

My answer is yes. Conceivably the individual could find the way himself, eventually, for he has within him all he needs, but most people have been confused by the mass consciousness and their egos. Exercised in falseness, they are leagues from clarity and so spun round they are unlikely to find themselves soon.

A woman once approached Master Yogananda on the matter of gurus, and what you say the woman also said.

"The term Self-realization," she declared, "appears to me to be totally incompatible with the Hindu belief concerning the need for a guru. I find Self-realization, as a concept, definitely attractive, but as a Westerner, I'm afraid I am put off by this 'guru' concept.

"I believe in standing on one's own two feet, in taking one's own hard knocks in life and learning one's lessons from them. What person of any character would want to gain his understanding in life through someone else?"

"What if you had your heart set on learning to pilot a plane?" Yogananda inquired. "Would you object to having someone show you how?"

"Well, obviously not," replied the woman, "but I'm talking about life situations, not artificial ones. What I mean is the sort of circumstance in which any grown-up ought to be able to make an adult decision."

"Surely it would be foolish to go through life without accepting advice from anyone," Yogananda said.

“Of course,” the lady agreed. “In the case of a guru, however, the disciple is forced to obey him without question, like a robot.”

“By no means!” replied Yogananda emphatically. “Any guru who demanded mindless obedience of his disciples would attract only mindless disciples. He would be given a wide berth by strong-willed devotees, who alone are fit for the path to God-realization.

“It takes great vigor, and great strength of character, to find God. Could the shock of omnipresence be sustained by spiritual weaklings?

“No disciple is forced to obey his guru. Freedom to accept or reject is one of the first laws of the spiritual life. It is a right given to us since the time of our creation by the Lord Himself.”

The Master smiled. “Just see how many people exercise their right to reject Him! . . . Yet the Lord is so humble, He never forces Himself on anyone. We may reject him for eons, and the Lord, while loving us through eternity, says, ‘I will wait.’

“Do you realize what you are saying when you are attracted to the concept, Self-realization, but reject the need for a guru? People commonly misunderstand Self-realization to mean the development of their human personality to its highest potential. But Self-realization is a soul-potential, not a human one.*

“The personality is like a dense forest, beyond which lies the beautiful, expansive land that God has promised you. To reach Him, you must somehow get out of the forest, and not waste time exploring its countless lanes.

* Yogananda meant – bound by our physicality and our conceptions of the possible, our humanness seriously lacks the infinite capacity of our Spirit.

"People have no idea how to get out of their mental forest. Every path they attempt ends in a confusion of dense undergrowth, or leads them back to where they first started out. In time, the realization dawns on them that they are lost.

"Then, if someone comes and says, 'I know this forest well; let me show you the way through it,' will they consider his offer a menace to their free will? Won't they view it, rather, as an opportunity to accomplish successfully what their own will has been trying for so long, but always in vain, to accomplish?

"You speak of adult decisions. In that forest, age has nothing to do with a person's ability to make a decision. Experience is what counts. Even a little child, if he knows the way, will lead you better than you can lead yourself, if you are lost. All of us, before God, are but children. Life itself is a great school, and our lessons in it won't end until we've realized who we really are, as children of the Infinite.

"The purpose of the guru is not to weaken your will. It is to teach you secrets of developing your inner power, until you can stand unshaken amidst the crash of breaking worlds.

"To develop such divine self-reliance is a much greater accomplishment, surely, than standing 'on your own two feet' in life's everyday situations.

"People who reject the need for a guru," Yogananda concluded, "don't realize what a steep mountain stands before them on the path to God. To climb this mountain without a guide would be worse than foolish: spiritually, it could prove disastrous."[1]

Fondly,

Anselam

Avatars Give Indirect Advice

Dear Arn,

Still you are troubled over gurus. Let me focus then on whether you need help to become self-realized.

A disciple once asked Master Maharaj your very question – "Is a guru inevitable?"

The Master replied, "It is like asking, 'Is a mother inevitable?'"[2]

To Sai Baba, the issue was simple: "A man struggling in a bog cannot be saved by another who is also caught in its slime. Only one standing on the firm ground can pull him out."[3]

The Mother, however, lived many years in France, and she understood your bent, Arn. "The Western mind always finds it difficult to submit totally to a Guru, and without total and unquestioning surrender to the Guru his help to you is paralyzed," she told the Academy. "That is why I generally advise westerners to find the guidance and the Presence within themselves; it is true that this process is very often open to uncertainty and self-deception, mistaking some voice of the ego in disguise for the Divine's guidance. In both cases, it is only an absolute sincerity and an unmixed humility that can be your safeguard."[4]

In the end, your treasure is within, said Baba. "Avatars seldom give advice directly. Whenever they wish to communicate, they convey more often by way of indirect suggestions and only rarely by direct method of instruction. The reason for this is there is divinity inherent in every human being, which he can manifest spontaneously if favourable conditions are provided, just as a viable seed will germinate and grow into a tree because of its inherent nature, if only suitable facilities are provided for the manifestation of its potentiality. Man should be enabled to correct himself by his own efforts, by merely giving timely suggestions rather than by stultifying his freedom and dignity through directives imposed from without. In short, the best maxim for helping people either in worldly matters or in the spiritual field is: '*Help them to help themselves' or 'Self-help is the best help*.'"[5]

Baba completely trusted the Power and Wisdom inherent in everyone, for it was the same Power and Wisdom *he* so completely displayed.

But surely the power of the teacher and the power of the student act together, Arn. Michelangelo, the Italian sculptor, coached his apprentice, the marble-hewer, with detailed instructions to "cut this way, level that, polish this." When done, the hewer was delighted – his sculpture was fine, and his appreciation, finer. "By your means," said he gratefully, "I have discovered a talent I did not know I possessed."[6]

Truly,

Anselam

Some Masters of the Academy

Dear Arn and Alma,

You both seek more about the Masters who taught me.

Because you are an intellectual and a rebel, Arn, start with a proven savant – Aurobindo. And because you are a woman and long for a woman's voice, Alma, start with Aurobindo's equal partner – Mirra Alfassa.

Aurobindo (1872-1950) was born a Bengali in Calcutta, India. He studied in England at St. Paul's and King's College, Cambridge, where he mastered English literature, French literature, Latin, Greek, Italian, German, and Spanish, and later he learned Sanskrit. A rare scholar, he was also to be a remarkable yogi.[7]

From 1900 to 1908, Aurobindo was a leading advocate of Indian independence. Feared by the British more than any other nationalist, he was arraigned with thirty-two others for "waging war against the king," that is, *high treason.*[8] Awaiting trial, he spent a year in the Alipore jail where he had a striking vision of the Divine in the form of Krishna, whom he saw in the "thieves, the murderers, the swindlers" of the prison, and in the prosecutor in the courtroom, and the judge too.[9] By then, Aurobindo had surrendered to his inner guide, who correctly assured him he would be released.

About to be re-arrested, he fled, heeding the voice, to Chandernagore in French India, then to Pondicherry, another French fragment in India, where he was safer from British designs. There he began an intense focus not on the liberation of his country, but on the liberation of humanity.

He sought the uplifting of human consciousness itself – a massive undertaking far beyond even the glow of self-realization.

Mirra Alfassa, born in Paris, France, in 1878, was inwardly highly evolved "even in childhood," Aurobindo wrote.[10] In her spiritual dreams and visions far from India, a luminous figure often appeared whom she called Krishna, and whom she recognized when first she saw him as Aurobindo. And Aurobindo in turn saw the power of the Divine Mother in her.

Mirra first met Aurobindo in Pondicherry in 1914, but the flowering of their spiritual collaboration began six years on, when she returned for life. In 1926, Aurobindo entrusted the ashram to her, and she became known affectionately as the Mother, while he went into seclusion for a quarter century to complete the task, he said, of transforming life "by bringing down into it the Light, Power and Bliss of the divine Truth and its dynamic certitudes."[11] In this time and earlier, he produced thirty volumes of writings. Before 1900, he had begun the 23 000 line poem, *Savriti: A Legend and a Symbol,* which he revised continually until his death in 1950.

A literato, Aurobindo knew well another Master of the Academy – Rabindranath Tagore (1861-1941), nobel prize winner for literature in 1913. "Tagore has been a wayfarer towards the same goal as ours in his own way – that is the main thing, the exact stage of advance and putting of the steps are minor matters," Aurobindo wrote.[12] In Tagore there was a "spiritual depth" and a "honeyladen felicity of expression" that could not be imitated "because they are things of the spirit and one must have the same sweetness and depth of soul before one can hope to catch any of these desirable qualities."[13] Surveying the multilingual panorama of poetry, Aurobindo reckoned: "At the subtlest elevation of all that has been reached stands or rather wings and floats in a high intermediate region the poetry of Tagore, not in the complete spiritual light, but amid an air shot with its seekings and glimpses, a sight and cadence found in a psycho-spiritual heaven of subtle and delicate soul experience transmuting the earth tones by the touch of its radiance."[14] In a new and discerning way, Tagore painted life, and he built "bridges of visioned light and rhythm between the infinite and eternal and the mind and soul and life of man."[15]

Another Indian Master, Nisargadatta Maharaj (1897-1981) was born in Bombay. Following the teachings of his guru unswervingly, he reached enlightenment and became a great teacher of the Advaita Vedanta philosophy, perhaps the greatest since Ramana Maharshi. His first name means "the one who dwells in the natural state."

If deep down that state was serene, it was not always so on the surface. Maharaj loved the cut and thrust of debate, he would shout at devotees, he seemed impatient, he abhorred people speaking of enlightenment who were not enlightened, he could be irascible, combative, dismissive, obnoxious. His approach reminds me how different these masters were from one another. But all of them had a power about them.

One day Edith Deri arrived reluctantly to "experience" Master Maharaj, expecting nothing if not a bad time.

Maharaj asked if she had any questions. She said no.

He asked why she had come.

"I have nothing to say," she answered. "I don't want to talk while I am here."

"But you must say something," said Maharaj. "Talk about anything you want to. Just say something."

"If I say something, you will then give some reply, and everyone will then applaud because you have given such a wonderful answer. I don't want to give you the opportunity to show off."

Untouched by the rudeness, Maharaj replied, "Water doesn't care whether it is quenching thirst or not."

This he repeated, slowly, as he did when saying something important.

Said David Godman, a student of Maharaj's, "Edith told me later that this one sentence completely destroyed her skepticism and her negativity. The words stopped her mind, blew away her determination to be a spoilsport, and put her into a state of peace and silence that lasted for long after her visit."[16]

Godman knew firsthand Maharaj's magic. Once, at the start of the monsoons, he waded through the floodwaters and sewer overflows, arriving at Maharaj's flat early. "I sat there in absolute silence with him for over an hour, and it was one of the most wonderful experiences I ever had with him," he recalled. "I felt an intense rock-solid silence descend on me that became deeper and deeper as the minutes passed. There was just a glow of awareness that filled me so completely, thoughts were utterly impossible. You don't realize what a monstrous imposition the mind is until you have lived without it, completely happily, completely silently, and completely effortlessly for a short period of time."[17] A testament it was to the power of the Master's aura, a power working in total silence.

Another time, Godman decided to argue with Maharaj, pointing to contradictions in his teaching. Usually, Maharaj relished such encounters, so he disputed Godman's claims awhile, then abruptly closed the conversation. "I don't think you really understand the purpose of my dialogues here," he said. "I don't say things simply to convince people that they are true. I am not speaking about these matters so that people can build up a philosophy that can be rationally defended, and which is free of all contradictions. When I speak my words, I am not speaking to your mind at all. I am directing my words directly at consciousness. I am planting my words in your consciousness. If you disturb the planting process by arguing about the meaning of the words, they won't take root there. Once my words have been planted in consciousness, they will sprout, they will grow, and at the appropriate moment they will bear fruit. It's nothing to do with you. All this will happen by itself. However, if you think about the words too much or dispute their meaning, you will postpone the moment of their fruition."

Scouring at Godman, he said severely, "Enough talking. Be quiet and let the words do their work!"[18]

Later, Godman asked if it mattered whether the words were actually heard or simply read, and Maharaj said, "The words will do their work whether you hear or read them. You can come here and listen to them in person, or you can read them in a book. If the teacher is enlightened, there will be a power in them."[19]

Truly,

Anselam

The words will do their work whether you hear or read them.

Nisargadatta Maharaj

Works of the Masters

Dear Arn,

Aha! A typical historian's question: what are the sources on Aurobindo, the Mother, Tagore and Maharaj?

The most comprehensive source on Aurobindo is the thirty volume Birth Centenary Library of *Collected Works,* published by the Sri Aurobindo Ashram Trust, Pondicherry, India. Aurobindo's voluminous writings are often difficult to penetrate due to his unique psychological and spiritual vocabulary, his massive scholarship, and his penchant for very long sentences that he deemed more able to bear the fullness of truth. Still, he could express tighter epigrams, as in his *Thoughts and Aphorisms* and in Pandit's several volumes of his distilled sayings. You might like Aurobindo, Arn, but he is a challenge. The Mother usually spoke in shorter, simpler phrases, and was an able translator of his curriculum and a magnificent teacher in her own right. The main sources on the Mother are the seventeen volume *Collected Works*, published by the Sri Aurobindo Ashram Trust and the thirteen volume *Mother's Agenda*, published by the Institute for Evolutionary Research. Her many insights are amply sown throughout these thirty volumes. Volumes 13, 14, and 15 of her *Collected Works*, also published separately as *Words* 1, 2, and 3, are particularly rewarding.

Numerous books exist on the teachings of Nisargadatta Maharaj, including Ramesh Balsekar's *Pointers from Nisargadatta Maharaj*, Jean Dunn's *Seeds of Consciousness - the Wisdom of Sri Nisargadatta Maharj,* and Robert Powell's *The Ultimate Medicine*, but the great classic, translated by

Maurice Frydman, is Sudhakar Dikshit's *I Am That - Talks with Sri Nisargadatta Maharaj.*

At least three of Rabindranath Tagore's writings represent the mystical side of this poetic Master – *Fireflies, Stray birds*, and *Gitangali.*

And a little on Sathya Sai Baba ... Born in 1926 in Puttaparti in southern India, he is a renowned healer and teacher. His miracles you can see in Howard Murphet's *Sai Baba: Man of Miracles* (1971), or *Sai Baba: Avatar* (1977), or in Erlendur Haraldsson's scholarly *Modern Miracles: An Investigative Inquiry . . .* (1997). Baba seems to know everyone's mind and past. He produces *vibhuti*, a curative holy ash, at will, and he has healed countless souls of numberless ailments, though not everyone is mended. He materializes rings and bracelets and necklaces that his devotees cherish forever. He has come to give people what they want, he says, so that they might want what he has to give. And that is simply – a reminder of Who they are.

More than four hundred fifty books in English alone exist by or about Sathya Sai Baba. At last tally, there were at least fourteen volumes of Baba's commentaries in *Summer Showers in Brindavan*, twenty-one volumes of his *Vahini* (Stream) series, and forty-one volumes of *Sathya Sai Speaks*. There are also abounding insights given by Baba to individual devotees.

A memorable Master of the Academy?

Yes, perhaps *the* most memorable . . . .

In Deep Appreciation,

Anselam

Being

Yogananda on the Healing Power of Thought

Dear Alma,

Yes, we are what we *think* we are – that is a good beginning, related to the feelings in your first letter and added to in your last.

Do you think you are a victim – unlistened to by your children, uninspired by your students, unappreciated by your colleagues, and unloved by Arn? You worry. You worry that the stock market has plunged five thousand points, your investments are decimated, your pension fund is endangered, your education fund for Larah and Sanson is halved, and now, not surprisingly, you worry about your health.

Yogananda (1893-1952) was a Master descended from a line of three other Masters. Sent by his guru to America to blend the highest ideals of Hinduism and Christianity, he personally introduced one hundred thousand people into Kriya yoga, and he created in California The Self-Realization Fellowship in 1920, a campus of the Academy that still exists. He wrote *Autobiography of a Yogi* (1946), a spiritual classic in any age.

Yogananda taught the power of thought.

He told a story of his teacher, Yukteswar, who was then learning at the feet of Master Mahasaya. A yogavatar, or Master of Masters, Lahiri Mahasaya asked about Yukteswar's health, and the latter complained of a serious illness and a growing loss of weight.

Mahasaya replied, "So you made yourself sick and now you think you are thin. But I am sure you will feel better tomorrow."

Next day, Yukteswar bounced to Mahasaya and declared, "Sir, with your blessings, I feel much better today."

"Your condition was indeed quite serious, and you are still frail," replied the Master. "Who knows how you might feel tomorrow?"

Next morning, Yukteswar moaned, "Sir, I am again ailing. I could hardly drag myself here to see you."

"So once more you indispose yourself," Mahasaya said.

Thus oscillated the days from health to ill-health until young Yukteswar realized that his expectations followed precisely his guru's suggestions.

"What is this?" said Mahasaya. "One day you say to me, 'I am well,' and the next day you say, 'I am sick.' It isn't that I have been healing or indisposing you. It is your own thoughts that have made you alternately weak and strong."

"If I think I am well and that I have regained my former weight, will it be so?" Yukteswar asked.

"It is so," Lahiri Mahasaya replied.

"At that very moment I felt both my strength and weight return," recalled Yukteswar. "When I reached my mother's home that night, she was startled to see my changed condition and thought I was swelling from dropsy. Many of my friends were so amazed at my sudden recovery that they became disciples of Lahiri Mahasaya."

Thus Yogananda learned from Yukteswar who learned from Mahasaya the power of thought.

"*Thought is the matrix of all creation; thought created everything*," stated Yogananda. "If you hold on to that truth with indomitable will, you can materialize any thought.

"Once you have said, 'I will,' never give in. If you say,

'I will never catch cold,' and the next morning you have a terrible cold and are discouraged, you are allowing your will to remain weak. You must not get discouraged when you see something happening that is contrary to what you have affirmed. Keep on believing, knowing it will be so. If outwardly you say, 'I will,' but inwardly think, 'I can't,' then you neutralize the power of thought and emasculate your will. If your will has become weakened by fighting disease or other reverses, you have to take the help of someone else's will to strengthen you through their prayers and positive affirmations on your behalf. But you must also do your part to change your consciousness."[1]

So, Alma, take a stand for yourself, reject illness, deny weakness, and activate your inner power of wholeness and vitality. Say, "this is how I shall be; this is the radiance I am; I accept nothing less."

Remember always Yogananda's promise to the Academy – "An unlimited source of protection for man lies in his strong thought that, as a child of God he cannot be affected by disease."[2] It would help someone as young as Sanson to know this, too.

Love,

Anselam

A Miracle Moment:

The Soft Inner Voice

Dear Alma,

You are absolutely right – the secret of taking a stand for yourself begins with a simple *choice*, Aala's gift, again.

What is the greatest choice you can make, you ask.

Listen to your Inner Voice.

Most people do not trust themselves enough to do so. It is the voice of Aala's Father whispering to you now, the voice of the Holy Spirit, the voice of Wisdom. Most people say they do not hear the voice, and some do not *want* to hear it, or even to hear *of* it. Most do not trust the only thing in their lives that is completely trustworthy. It is a denial of their innermost reality, but denial is the choice of many.

This inner voice speaks gently because it knows you may be afraid, even of yourself. Jesus of *A Course in Miracles* says, "The Voice of the Holy Spirit does not command, because it is incapable of arrogance. It does not demand, because it does not seek control. It does not overcome, because it does not attack. It merely reminds."[3] And when you hear and heed, Aala's Father Himself is grateful. Remember, says Jesus, "An unheard message will not save the world, however mighty be the Voice that speaks, however loving may the message be."[4]

Have you read "The Golden Crane" in the third volume of *Chicken Soup for the Soul*?

At the LaFarge Lifelong Learning Institute in Milwaukee, Wisconsin, Art Beaudry was an expert in the ancient Japanese craft of origami, or paper folding.

About to take scores of paper cranes to a mall display, Art heard a voice telling him to make a crane out of golden foil. When he resisted, the voice said, "Do it! And you must give it away tomorrow to a special person."

"What person?" Art asked.

"You will know which one."

So Art shaped the delicate, golden bird and took it to the mall.

The next day dozens of interested people learned the intricacies of crane-folding. Then suddenly, a woman stood before Art, and he reached for the golden one.

"I don't know why, but there's a voice inside me telling me I'm supposed to give you this golden crane," said Art. "The crane is the ancient symbol of peace."

The woman caressed the beautiful bird in her hand, as tears filled her eyes.

"My husband died three weeks ago," she whispered. "This is the first time I've been out . . . Today."

Wiping her face, she said, "Today is our wedding anniversary."

Then she added assuredly, "Now I know that my husband is at peace . . . It's the most wonderful fiftieth wedding anniversary present I could have received. Thank you for listening to your heart."[5]

To Listening,

Anselam

More Voice

Dear Alma,

May I say more about the Voice? And about Aala?

Aala lived for centuries in those early times, and her children and grand children and great grandchildren and great great grandchildren numbered in the hundreds. Before she died, she lamented to her Father that the youngest generation were no longer listening to their inner voice. Some had said it was too quiet to hear, and others said they couldn't hear what didn't exist. What they did hear was the increasing cacophony of outer voices, especially their own.

"My children sleep," said her Father, "and must be awakened."

"How?" asked Aala.

"With the very Voice they say they cannot hear."

This puzzled Aala, so her Father waited, then spoke again.

"How can you wake children in a more kindly way than by a gentle Voice that will not frighten them, but will merely remind them that the night is over and the light has come? You do not inform them that the nightmares that frightened them so badly are not real, because children believe in magic. You merely reassure them that they are safe now. Then you train them to recognize the difference between sleeping and waking, so that they will understand they need not be afraid of dreams. And so when bad dreams come, they will themselves call on the light to dispel them.

"A wise teacher teaches through approach, not avoidance. He does not emphasize what you must avoid to escape from harm, but what you need to learn to have joy. Consider the fear and confusion a child would experience if he were told, 'Do not do this because it will hurt you and make you unsafe; but if you do that instead, you will escape from harm and be safe, and then you will not be afraid.' It is surely better to say only three words: 'Do only that!' This simple statement is perfectly clear, easily understood and very easily remembered."[6]

"Should we tell my great grandchildren and their children the huge mistake they have made?" asked Aala.

"I think not," said her Father, recalling especially the little ones and the nature of His Holy Spirit, which was after all, the Voice.

Said He, "The Holy Spirit never itemizes errors because He does not frighten children, and those who lack wisdom *are* children. Yet He always answers their call, and His dependability makes them more certain."[7]

Fondly,

Anselam

Education and its Purpose

Dear Alma,

You say education should be about listening to your heart, but your colleagues do not know what that means. You say education is the study of all you can be, the study of your real nature, the uncovering of your inner beauty, living your life as Spirit, expressing yourself as Love and Joy – the fulfillment of your highest conception of self. You say these matters ought to be the core of education . . .

You are not far off the viewpoint of Master Baba. "Education is not for mere living; it is for life, a fuller life, a more meaningful, a more worthwhile life," said he. "There is no harm if it is also for a gainful employment, but the educated must be aware that existence is not all, that gainful employment is not all. Again, education is not for developing the faculty of argument, criticism, or winning a polemic victory over your opponents or exhibiting your mastery over language or logic. That study is the best which teaches you to conquer this cycle of birth and death, which gives you the mental equipoise that will not be affected by the prospect of death, that will not be disturbed by the blessings or blows of Fate. That study begins where this study of yours ends."[8]

Equipoise, Alma, so important for your school system that cultivates it so ineptly, and for you, with all your worries . . . You are like P.G. Wodehouse's golfer: "The least thing upset him on the links. He missed short putts because of the uproar of butterflies in the adjoining meadows."[9]

To Love of Self,

Anselam

P.S. You may show this letter to Arn, the golfer, and to Arn, the scholar, who in grad school developed the faculty of argument and criticism that troubles him still.

An Argument over Details

Dear Alma,

Your argument seems unnecessary. You take the stance of the highest vision, the search for the greatness of the Self, the ideals of the Academy, and your angry colleague is interested in petty detail, in mundane minutiae, you say . . .

One day at Pondicherry campus of the Academy, the Mother spoke of this very issue.

"In education, both tendencies should be encouraged side by side: the tendency to thirst for the marvelous, for what seems unrealizable, for something which fills you with the feeling of divinity; while at the same time encouraging exact, correct, sincere observation in the perception of the world as it is, the suppression of all imagination, a constant control, a highly practical and meticulous sense for exact details. Both should go side by side. Usually you kill the one with the idea that this is necessary in order to foster the other – this is completely wrong. Both can be simultaneous, and there comes a time when one has enough knowledge to know that they are the two aspects of the same thing: insight, a higher discernment.

"From the point of view of education, this would be very important: to see the world as it is, exactly, unadorned, in the most down-to-earth and concrete manner; and to see the world as it can be, with the freest, highest vision, the one most full of hope and aspiration and marvelous certitude – as the two poles of discernment.

"The most splendid, most marvelous, most powerful, most expressive, most total things we can imagine are nothing compared to what they can be; and at the same time our meticulous exactitude in the tiniest detail is never exact enough. And both must go together. When one knows this (*downward gesture*) and when one knows that (*upward gesture*), one is able to put the two together."[10]

Anthony De Mello, the Catholic writer, told a story in *The Song of the Bird* of the importance of your colleague's position.

Constant Awareness

No Zen student would presume to teach
others until he had lived with his
master for at least ten years.

Tenno, having completed his ten years
of apprenticeship, acquired the rank of teacher.
One day he went to visit the master
Nan-in. It was a rainy day, so Tenno
wore wooden clogs and carried an
umbrella.

When he walked in, Nan-in greeted him
with, "You left your wooden clogs
and umbrella on the porch, didn't
you? Tell me, did you place your
umbrella on the right side of the
clogs or on the left?"

> Tenno was embarrassed, for he did not know
> the answer. He realized he lacked
> awareness. So he became Nan-in's student
> and labored for another ten years
> to acquire constant awareness.[11]

Alma, it is now winter where you live, and the roads are icy, and gravel trucks have spread sand and small rocks to help you drive. Have you noticed a little thing when passing cars – most of the gravel is in the centre of the road, and when you cut in too quickly after overtaking a car, you shower rocks onto its windshield? To avoid the damage, all you need do is notice that your tires throw up rocks when you drive over gravel . . . a little thing . . . but most people don't realize what they are doing until the big thing, the shower of sand and stone.

The big is in the little; the vastness, in the speck. Similarly, the divine is everywhere, and you miss it if you do not see it in the mundane, in the detail. Remember Horton in *Horton Hears a Who!* – the loyal elephant who sees an infinity in a wee Who; who sees the sea in a scintilla?

Does not your love find expression in little things? And if it be truly love, does it ever overlook anything, any opportunity to support and sweeten, to touch and to transform? Your colleague may or may not understand your viewpoint, but you can understand hers.

To Big and Small,

Anselam

P.S. Not all Catholics deem De Mello a saint. Some declaim against his admiration of Moslem, Jewish, and Hindu mystics, judging that such praise does not a Catholic make, but his magnificent liberality, his all-inclusiveness, a *saint* they do suggest.

Company of the Good

Dear Larah,

I am so pleased you have two very close friends, so loyal to each other, so helpful. You are right – it makes a great difference who your friends are, especially at your age.

Sai Baba always emphasized the people around us.

"You are shaped by the company you keep," he said: "a piece of iron turns into rust if it seeks the company of the soil. It glows, it softens and takes on useful shapes if it enjoys the company of fire. Dust can fly if it chooses the wind as its friend; it has to end as slime in a pit if it prefers water. It has neither wing nor foot, yet it can either fly or walk, rise or fall, according to the friend it selects.[12]

"A cup of water has no cash value, but if it is poured into ten cups of milk it acquires the value that people attach to milk. If, on the other hand, one cup of milk is poured into ten cups of water, it loses the value it had and is condemned as useless."[13]

Do all you can to help your friends see the charm of their inner beauty, Larah, and remember your own too, no matter how small you may feel.

Wonderful! Your mother has read *Horton Hears a Who!* to little Sanson.

Love,

Anselam

Mixed Company

Dear Alma and Arn,

I was just answering Larah about how important her friends were, a fact she had first mentioned to *me*! Good for her! Mixed company can have surprising effects, as you know.

There was a woman who had two female parrots who constantly squawked, "Hi, we're prostitutes. Want to have some fun?" The owner was always embarrassed. Every time someone visited, the parrots would shout together, "Hi, we're prostitutes! Want to have some fun?" Exasperated, the woman went to her minister, who just happened to have two perfectly behaved male parrots. One read the Bible every day, and the other had a string of prayer beads and prayed all day long. "Don't worry," said the minister. "I know how to reform your parrots. We'll place them in with my two parrots where they can learn reverence and self-control."

So the woman agreed, and placed her two loose females in the cage with the two strict males. Immediately, the two females shouted, "Hi, we're prostitutes! Want to have some fun?"

Then the parrot with the Bible said to his partner, "Put away the beads, Roy. Our prayers have been answered!"

Share this with Larah, if appropriate. She is older than her years, and she has a delightful sense of humor.

Cheers,

Anselam

Dharmaraja in Hell

Dear Alma, Arn, and Larah,

Being in the company of even one enlightened soul can be enough. Consider that the average person does not meet one individual in her whole life who has decided that self-realization is her main purpose here, not one.[14]

Master Sai Baba sometimes preceded a saying with a story, a technique to embed the truth in memory. "The services to man are more valuable than what you call 'Services to God,'" he said. "God has no need of your service. Please man you please God."[15] A story about the struggle between good and evil, between the Pandavas and their corrupted cousins, the Kauravas, prefaces that statement:

"Dharmaraja, the eldest of the Pandavas," said Baba, "was a sincere adherent of *Sathya* [Truth]. But, during the Kurukshethra battle, he was persuaded to utter a white lie, a subterfuge which he thought was excusable, though it was not [one hundred] percent honest. In order to kill Drona, the master archer and General on the opposite side, they had to somehow trick him into discarding his bow; so they planned a subterfuge. They named a war elephant after Drona's son, Aswatthama. Then, they killed it. Immediately, within the hearing of Drona, the Pandava army was asked to shout in glee, 'Aswatthama is killed – the elephant,' which was strictly true. But, while the soldiers were repeating the words, 'the elephant,' drums were beaten, bugles were sounded, trumpets pealed, so that

Drona heard only the first three words. Naturally, he took them to mean that his son had met with his death from enemy hands. Drona was heavily laden with grief; his hands could not wield the bow and the arrow, as deftly as usual; at that moment, he was overwhelmed and slain. For this one sin that he had encouraged, the only one in his life, Dharmaraja had to spend a few minutes in Hell, say the *Puranas* [Hindu scriptures]. Such is the consequence of departing from [Truth] even by a hair's breadth.

"Listen to the sequel. When the emissaries of the other world were escorting Dharmaraja after death to Hell, for this nominal sojourn, the denizens of Hell suddenly felt a coolness and a fragrance in the air they breathed, a strange peace and joy, a thrill and exhilaration which they had never hoped to enjoy. That was the consequence of the holy soul approaching the region of terror and torture. The unfortunate sinners gathered around Dharmaraja to be soothed and comforted by his very sight. When Dharmaraja was directed to turn back towards Heaven (the term of his sentence was soon over) the populace of Hell cried out to him to prolong his stay. They were reluctant to go back to the heat and the pain. Hearing their piteous wail, Dharmaraja declared that he was surrendering to them all the merit that had earned Heaven for him; he was willing to stay with them! But that great act of renunciation not only benefited the suffering creatures, it gave Dharmaraja a greater lease of life in Heaven and a more honoured place there. Life is best spent in alleviating pain, assuaging distress, and promoting peace and joy.

"The service of man is more valuable than what you call 'service to God.' God has no need of your service. Please man; you please God."[16] When you serve man, you serve God.

And equally important, the company of a single enlightened soul is enough to brighten your outlook, even the entire outlook of masses in torment. Not *several* good men or women; *one* suffices.

Blessings,

Anselam

We are awaiting the long-promised invasion.

So are the fishes.

Winston Churchill, broadcast, to the defeated French, 1940

Determination and Desire and Focus

Dear Arn,

Let me re-emphasize the level of sincerity required to move into your Power constantly. Of course, you need to trust your teacher and to trust yourself, but as Maharaj noted, "merely to trust is not enough. You must also desire. Without desire for freedom of what use is the confidence that you can acquire freedom? Desire and confidence must go together."[17]

And the desire must be an unrelenting determination, not a passing fancy.

Two stories might appeal to your historian's heart, Arn. Philip, father of Alexander the Great, had all but subdued the Greek city-states when at last he approached Sparta, politely at first, then sternly. "You are advised to submit without further delay," he threatened, "for if I bring my army into your land, I will destroy your farms, slay your people, and raze your city."

The Spartans deliberated a moment, then answered – "If."

Mindful of Sparta's military renown and determination, Philip thought better and left the city alone.[18]

After the fall of France in 1940, Winston Churchill broadcast by radio to the French: "We are awaiting the long-promised invasion. So are the fishes."[19]

Mindful of Churchill's candor, Hitler desisted, and while he did not leave the British alone, he turned eastward.

Iron determination bears no compromises. "Nothing can block you so effectively as compromise, for it shows lack of earnestness, without which nothing can be done," said Master Maharaj.[20] You are not compromising on becoming one hundred percent Spirit, or on discarding your ego completely, or deleting your martyrdom fully. "The desire to find the self [and to be the Power and Wisdom] will be surely fulfilled, provided you want nothing else," said Maharaj. "But you must be honest with yourself and really want nothing else. If in the meantime you want many other things and are engaged in their pursuit, your main purpose may be delayed until you grow wiser and cease being torn between contradictory urges. Go within, without swerving, without ever looking outward."[21]

There is another part to this unbending determination, this steely sincerity – it is neither impatient nor arrogant. "Fix not the time and the way in which the ideal shall be fulfilled," said Aurobindo. "Work and leave time and way to God all-knowing . . . Work as if the ideal had to be fulfilled swiftly and in thy lifetime; persevere as if thou knewest it not to be unless purchased by a thousand years yet of labour. That which thou darest not expect till the fifth millennium, may bloom out with tomorrow's dawning and that which thou hopest and lustest after now, may have been fixed for thee in thy hundredth advent."

To become Spirit and to allow the Power and Wisdom in us to be us, know the right attitude, said the Mother: "as much energy and ardour as if we were certain of achieving it in our present life, as much patience and endurance as if we needed centuries to realize it."[22]

Spirit to be Spirit must be free to act in a second or an eon. Aurobindo, in his typical, jolting way, declared: "I am weary of the childish impatience which cries and blasphemes and denies the ideal because the Golden Mountains cannot be reached in our little day or in a few momentary centuries."[23]

Determination undissuaded by centuries, if centuries be needed, is precisely what real determination means.

Can you see, Arn, that your sincerity must be impregnable, insuperable?

To Determination,

Anselam

P.S. Sanson, with his toy soldiers, might be interested in Philip and the Spartans and Churchill and the war.

Movie Humor

Dear Alma and Arn,

Persistence, determination, discipline, unbroken focus, uninterrupted ardor, unrelenting toil, undivided sincerity: these qualities strain and stress, you both say. Is there no relief, you wonder, no lighter side, no amusement to self-realization?

Yes, the more evolved you become, the more important is your sense of humor.

Look for it, express it, freely and often.

You both love films and know of Sam Goldwyn (1882-1974), an early movie mogul.

One day a copy of *The Making of Yesterday: The Diaries of Raoul de Roussy de Sales, 1938-1942*, landed on Goldwyn's desk as a prospective movie. Astounded, Goldwyn, exclaimed, "How do you like that? Four years old and the kid keeps a diary!"[24]

Goldwyn always bragged that he had the world's finest literary giants on retainer. Once, he attracted Maurice Maeterlinck – the celebrated Belgian Nobel Prize winner, and author of the classic *The Life of the Bee* – to Hollywood. Maeterlinck arrived with dollar signs in his eyes and a deep angst that he knew nothing of movies. "I know you don't understand motion-picture technique," Goldwyn soothed. "That doesn't matter. All I want you to do is just go away and write your greatest book over in the form of a scenario."

Relieved, Maeterlinck whisked away, and returned triumphantly weeks later with the blockbuster. Elated,

Goldwyn retired to his office to read the masterwork. Minutes later, he burst into the foyer screaming: "My God! The hero is a bee!"[25]

Director William Wyler had been trying vainly to explain a certain scene to Goldwyn. Again and again he tried, to no avail. Confounded, he turned to Goldwyn's son, age fifteen, and blurted, "Do *you* understand it, Sammy?"

"Sure," said the boy. "It's perfectly clear to me."

"Since when are we making pictures for kids?" grunted Goldwyn.[26]

Another time, Goldwyn had a ghostwriter pen some articles supposedly by the movie maestro himself. Part way through, the writer got sick, and a substitute was found, but the results lacked sparkle. Depressed, Goldwyn said, "That's not at all up to my usual standard." [27]

Perhaps this story will appeal to your little plagiarizers, Alma, and your bigger ones, Arn.

To Humor,

Anselam

Churchill's Compassion

Dear Arn,

Why not use history to inspire? In it is more than doom, death and destruction.

In summer 1941, Sergeant James Allen Ward was 13 000 feet over the Zuider Zee when the starboard engine of his Wellington bomber caught fire. Roped about his waist, he crawled onto the wing in the gale and doused the flames, and then somehow inched back to the cockpit. He was awarded the Victoria Cross for heroism and summoned to 10 Downing Street, where Churchill waited expectantly. But, out of his element completely, Ward was speechless and could not answer a single question.

Seeing the New Zealander's discomfort, Churchill said, "You must feel very humble and awkward in my presence."

"Yes, sir," mumbled Ward.

"Then you can imagine how humble and awkward I feel in yours," said Churchill."[28]

To Heroes,

Anselam

The Infinite Value of a Comma

Dear Alma and Arn,

An example that relates to your recent letter about details, Alma, and one that might appeal to your grammarian's sensibilities, Arn . . .

Some people are not sticklers for punctuation, but I am, when it matters.

Maria Fedorovna, 1847-1928, was empress of Russia, wife of Czar Alexander III and daughter of King Christian IX of Denmark. After the Revolution of 1918, she wisely returned to her homeland.

She was a kind person, and known for her kindness. She once rescued a prisoner from a frozen fate in Siberia by transposing a little comma in a warrant signed by the czar. Her husband had written, "Pardon impossible, to be sent to Siberia." But Maria moved the comma one word to the left, so the warrant now read: "Pardon, impossible to be sent to Siberia." The prisoner was freed.[29]

I have sent this to Larah, who is dismayed by punctuation rules.

Love,

Anselam

P.S. I am happy you are feeling better. Yes, *choose* your attitude and stand by it! That is being loyal to yourself.

Pardon, impossible
to be sent
to Siberia

Two Officers After the German Surrender

Dear Arn,

Another upbearing tale regarding your war interests, from the British actor David Niven . . .

Just after Germany's surrender in 1945, Niven passed a farm wagon in that ruined country.

"I glanced casually at the two men sitting up behind the horse. Both wore typical farmer headgear and sacks were thrown over their shoulders protecting them from a light drizzle. We were just past them when something made me slam on the brakes and back up. I was right, the man who was not driving was wearing field boots. I slipped out from behind the wheel, pulled my revolver from its holster and told the corporal to cover me with his Tommy gun.

"I gestured to the men to put their hands over their heads and told them in fumbling German to produce their papers.

"'I speak English,' said the one with the field boots, 'this man has papers – I have none.'

"'Who are you?' I asked.

"He told me his name and rank – 'General.'

"'We are not armed,' he added, as I hesitated.

"Sandhurst [British Army officer training] did it – I saluted, then motioned to them to lower their hands.

"'Where are you coming from, sir?'

"He looked down at me. I had never seen such utter weariness, such black despair on a human face before.

He passed a hand over the stubble of his chin.

"'Berlin,' he said quietly.

"'Where are you going, sir?'

"He looked ahead down the road towards the village and closed his eyes.

"'Home,' he said almost to himself, 'it's not far now . . . only . . . one more kilometer.'

"I didn't say anything. He opened his eyes again and we stared at each other. We were quite still for a long time. Then I said, 'Go ahead, sir,' and added ridiculously . . . 'please cover up your bloody boots.'

"Almost as though in pain, he closed his eyes and raised his head, then with sobbing intake of breath, covered his face with both hands and they drove on."[30]

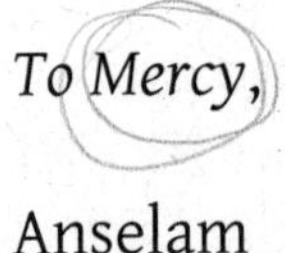

To Mercy,

Anselam

Master Krishnamurti

Dear Arn,

Yes, seek *examples* of love, as opposed to *precepts* about love, however touching. You wanted an example from one of the Masters of the Academy.

Jiddu Krishnamurti (1895-1986) was a great teacher who spoke to enthralled audiences the world over. A Master who told people to reject Masters, an authority who urged them to shun authority, he turned all seekers inward to the Truth in themselves.

Krishnamurti, a sister student reminded me, "always had this strange lack of distance between himself and the trees, rivers and mountains. It wasn't cultivated: you can't cultivate a thing like that. There was never a wall between him and another. What they did to him, what they said to him never seemed to wound him, nor flattery to touch him. Somehow he was altogether untouched."[31]

"You asked me just now about personal love," Krishnamurti once told a student, "and my answer is that I no longer know it. Personal love does not exist for me. Love is for me a constant inner state. People sometimes think that I am superficial and cold. But it is not indifference, it is merely a feeling of love that is constantly within me and that I simply cannot help giving to everyone that I come into touch with."[32] "The sun does not care upon whom it shines," he said. "It shines for all."[33]

At Ehrwald, Switzerland, in 1923, a friend watched Krishnamurti: "He was lying amongst the long grass and flowers when a butterfly settled on his hand, and soon he had one or two poised on his finger. His delight was unbounded. He has a love of all creatures great and small, indeed anything that is beautiful or natural interests him; he will chase a grasshopper following its movements and noting the colour of its wings; or with his customary, 'I say!' will stand almost enraptured before a beautiful scene. 'Just look at that lake, it's so smooth, like ice – and dark green. See the reflections on it? Oh-ee, you should see Lake Geneva – so blue.'"[34]

One morning in the Academy residences, Krishnamurti was alone, writing in his room with the window open. Suddenly he felt peering eyes behind him. Turning, he beheld a full-grown langur monkey in the window, watching him with unbroken focus. Krishnamurti rose and walked toward the visitor, and when he stopped face to face, the monkey held out its hand. Krishnaji took it gently, and they held each other for some minutes. "There was complete trust," said a friend. "Krishnaji describes the touch of the palm as strong, infinitely soft, despite calluses which had formed from climbing branches." Sensing a larger welcome, the monkey then attempted to move in, but Krishnamurti gently but firmly pushed him back and shut the window.[35]

So it was the *example* of the Master's love that impressed and taught us.

To Examples,

Anselam

Master Baba

Dear Arn,

Yes, there are illustrations from Baba too.

One day years ago, a group of devotees took Sai Baba to the jungle, then full of deer. Said one, "About four or five deer came near to our jeep, and I said that if I had a gun I would shoot them. Swami [Baba] felt so bad about this that he did not eat for two days. From that day onwards we stopped shooting deer."[36]

When Baba was young, his schoolmates would punish him for knowing the answer to the teacher's questions. "If he gave the answer the boys would beat him," said Baba, referring to himself. "If he did not give it, the teacher would beat him." Sometimes the pupil who had answered correctly had to slap the faces of those who did not. "Since Swami [Baba] was small, he had to stand on a chair to slap. But he would slap gently. Then the teacher would slap him hard as many times as he had slapped gently." Seeing these things, Baba's schoolmates grew affectionate.[37]

To Gentleness,

Anselam

P.S. You may share this with Alma, Larah and little Sanson.

Love is Being Completely Present

Dear Alma,

Part of your difficulty stems from multi-tasking, a current buzzword suggesting erroneously that you can be several places at once, address several issues at once, and listen to several people at once. When you try to be present in four or five or six places simultaneously, chances are that you are present in none of them for more than an interrupted second. Love, to be itself, cannot be intermittent, on again, off again, like a broken current.

Recently an adventurer risked life and limb fording rivers and crossing mountains to visit the sixteenth Karmapa, a holy Tibetan lama. Intently and lovingly, the Karmapa greeted the guest as if he were a last friend, or a long-absent son. The affection and attention were undistractable, undisturbable – because the lama was totally *present*.

Sharon Salzberg, a Buddhist student of the Academy, had a similar experience. She was on crutches, recovering from a grave car accident when a distinguished visitor arrived at her spiritual retreat – the Dalai Lama. Streets were barricaded, troopers manned the roofs, and the retreat resembled a fortress. Lost on the fringes was Salzberg, feeling apart and alone as the huge crowd surged forward. "The Dalai Lama got out, looked around, and saw me standing way in the back of the throng, leaning on the crutches," said Salzberg. "He cut straight through the crowd and came up to me, as though he were homing in on

the deepest suffering in the situation. He took my hand, looked me in the eye, and asked 'What happened?'"[38]

He too was completely present, Alma.

To Attentiveness,

Anselam

Sayings on Love

Dear Alma,

I concede your point. There is more in a saying than just words, more in an axiom than just a rule. You are wise to remind me that Master Maharaj said as much. A maxim expressed by a truth-teller is a gift of wisdom and love; it is the *energy* of those powers, and so it is always alive. An excellent insight!

And it needs to be *said* from time to time, as there are many who will miss your drift if it is only conveyed by example, however comely.

What are my favorite sayings on love?

A hard choice, but here are a few I heard from different Masters of the Academy:

> The most important thing you have to develop is love. If you develop love, you don't have to develop anything else.[39]

Sai Baba

> The Grace of God cannot be won through the gymnasium of reason, the contortions of yoga or the denials of asceticism. Love alone can win it, Love that needs no requital, Love that knows no bargaining, Love that is unwavering. Love alone can overcome obstacles, however many or mighty.[40]

Sai Baba

Soft, sweet speech is the expression of genuine love.
Hate screeches, fear squeals, conceit trumpets.
But love sings lullabies, it soothes, it applies balm.
Practice the vocabulary of love, and unlearn
the language of hate and contempt.[41]

Sai Baba

Hislop : How does one see God Himself?
In order to see the moon, does one need a torch?
It is by the light of the moon that one sees the moon.
In like fashion, if one wishes to see God, it is by love,
which is the light of God, that one may see Him.[42]

Sai Baba

Do not beat your children – It clouds *your*
consciousness and spoils *their* character.[43]

The Mother

The Rungs of Love
At first one loves only when one is loved.
Next, one loves spontaneously, but one wants to
be loved in return.
Then one loves even if one is not loved, but one
still wants one's love to be accepted.
And finally one loves purely and simply,
without any other need or joy than that of loving.[44]

The Mother

Let yourself feel deeply and totally the power of love . . . Use key words: it's *safe* to feel the potency of love, I am *protected* in the feeling of the power of love, I am *strong* in the feeling or emotion of love, there is a *gentleness* in the feeling, a peace.[45]

Larry Wayne & Grace Johnston

These are my favorites because of how they make me feel. Elevated, their essence is known even to very young children.

Love,

Anselam

P.S. Good that you shared the letter about the Dalai Lama and Salzberg with Arn, and that Arn seems less distant.

Rising to the Level of Student Expectations

Dear Alma,

You have a student teacher in your classroom, and the young woman has just watched *Stand and Deliver*, the movie about Jaime Escalante, the superb math teacher at Garfield High School, Los Angeles, some years ago. The novice repeated enthusiastically Escalante's mantra – "Students will rise to the level of expectations." True, not because they follow blindly any pied piper, but because progressively higher realizations are natural to them. And this natural affinity is so apparent, so compelling, that the opposite of Escalante's mantra is also true – teachers can rise to the level of *student* expectations.

Ask even your grade twos or threes what a great teacher is, and they will tell you in simpler words what a master teacher is and does. They will say, "She loves us, she cares about us, she is kind, she is happy, she smiles, she is calm, she is fussy about some things, she helps us when we hurt, she holds us when we cry . . ."

Ask your student teacher to pursue her insight about expectations further. Suggest that she ask her little ones what their expectations are, what they think good teachers are, and if she takes their response to heart, she might rise to the level of *their* high hopes. You see, a child is usually not so manipulative as to have an expectation. He simply knows what makes him feel right.

Then I might recommend focusing on your own expectations of yourself.

Love,

Anselam

Larah and Sanson

Dear Larah,

You are like a second mother to little Sanson. My own mother was a second mother to her younger brother too, as he recalled tearfully after she died at age eighty-nine. Baba said you can repay many debts, but the one "to your mother you can never repay."[46]

Sanson, you say, is bright like his father and can already read. Encourage him to be loving like his mother – so that he will know *what* to read, and so that his intelligence is always guided by affection, by his good feeling for himself, and his wishing well for others. Help him to see the Spirit in all people and all things, and help him to be kind to both. Help him to love a tall cedar, a tender tulip, help him to love love and wonder and kindness, creativeness, positiveness, happiness, determination, enthusiasm, laughter and joy. Help him to feel these energies alive and in him. Above all, help him to think well of himself, to see himself as Spirit, a child of the Great Spirit. Teach him to welcome the Great Spirit within him, to hear it, heed it, be it.

In so doing, be a beautiful example to *yourself*, Larah, inspire *yourself*, and if that inspires others, including your mother, so much the better.

Love,

Anselam

P.S. Sanson's name comes from Hebrew and means Sun; yours comes from Latin and means Cheerful.

Prince

Dear Larah,

You might tell this story to Sanson when you read to him at night.

An Irish soldier lived with his wife and his little dog, Prince, in Hammersmith, London, before he was shipped to France in 1914 when the Great War began. The soldier returned on brief leave, then left again for the trenches. But when his master went this time, Prince was dispirited, refused to eat, then left home. For ten days, the wife searched, but found nothing, and finally she wrote sadly to her husband at Armentieres, saying Prince was gone for good. Then she was astounded to discover that the dog was in France! Prince had somehow legged it seventy miles to the coast, somehow crossed the English Channel, and somehow weaved sixty more miles, the last under murderous bombardment and clouds of poison gas, and then among millions of soldiers had found his master.

How did Prince do it? What drew him through all the distance and all the danger to his master?[47]

Ask Sanson.

Fondly,

Anselam

Loving Things

Dear Larah,

So, young Sanson said Prince went to all that trouble, because he "liked his owner very much." I think so – it was love that drew the dog to his master.

Most people have no idea of the power of love. It can affect anything and everything.

Sanson already has a computer and knows more about it than your father. I understand that your dad is one of twenty-five percent of all people with computers who have *physically attacked* their computer! I wonder what your father thinks of his computer, and I wonder what Sanson thinks of his, and I wonder if little Sanson might instruct his father on the right attitude?

You see, little Sanson actually loves his computer. And loving makes a difference, and not just to the one who loves.

Years ago when my car broke down, I met a strange mechanic who was a sort of car doctor. He said cars could actually sense his feelings about them, and he worked with them as if they had a mind of their own, a mind that responded to deep caring. He listened quietly, respectfully, and the car seemed to point to the problem. Then he labored gently and lovingly and fixed the problem. And the car actually seemed grateful that someone had at last seen it as something more than a ton of metal.

A fellow student of the Academy once told of an old hospital janitor he knew who repaired watches as a hobby and who loved gadgetry that worked to perfection. Whenever an instrument in the hospital malfunctioned, they would call Robert, and often as soon as he appeared it would begin working again. Sometimes it waited for his benign hand before re-starting. Late one night, a cardiac monitor froze, and the nurse urgently ordered, "Call Robert!" The moment he arrived, the monitor turned on.[48]

French researcher Rene Peoc'h created a little robot, whom he called Tychoscope 1, and programmed it to move across a space randomly, so it was in each part of the space the same length of time. Then he conditioned newborn chicks to adopt the robot as their mother. He wanted to see if the natural attraction of the chicks for their mother would make the robot spend more time near them. Indeed, Tychoscope spent two and half times longer near "her" children than when she was in the cage all by herself. There was less than one chance in a thousand this difference was due to chance.[49] What drew the robot to the chicks? Something in the bonding most likely. Love?

When the robot stayed away, possibly the squabbling of the chicks, due to fluke combinations of ones naturally dominant, overrode the love-call to their "mother," much in the same way that human struggles for dominance drown out the public good.

In 1968, Dr. John Hislop was interviewing Sathya Sai Baba when he noticed water dripping from a box holding four beautiful Indian saris. Of one hundred, Baba had selected ninety-six as gifts to lady volunteers, leaving these four to be returned to the seller. No source of water lay near, so Hislop and others were puzzled.

"The saris are weeping because Swami has rejected them," said Baba.

"Swami! How could that be?" asked Hislop. "Does Swami say that inanimate objects have injured feelings and can weep?"

"Inanimate objects are also capable of feeling joy and grief," said Baba, who then took the saris gently and gave them to Mrs. Hislop and three other ladies. "There is nothing in this world which has no heart, which is incapable of feeling joy or grief!" Baba added later. "Only, you must have the eye to see, the ear to listen, the heart to respond."[50]

Larah, have you heard of the "pathetic fallacy" in your English classes? Your father knows of it. When writers give human qualities to things not human, they are said to use the pathetic fallacy. But the only thing pathetic about the fallacy is that it *is* a pathetic fallacy.

Warmly,

Anselam

Can You Determine Your Emotions?

Dear Alma,

What you say, others have said too: "love is beautiful, love transforms, love heals, and resolves, but love is hard to come by. You can't just materialize it; it comes and goes, like the wind; and you can't make the wind blow . . ."

You ask if I am able to determine my emotions.

Yes, with three in particular – positivity, joy, and love. For each I developed a breathing strategy. For positivity, with each in-breath I imagined thousands of little plus signs materializing in my body, the power source, and when I breathed out, I cast all these plus signs on everything outside of me. So everything was imbued with this delightful sense of positivity.

And because the power source in me was inexhaustible, when I breathed out, the concentration of plus signs within was instantly and automatically replenished. That is, the act of giving positivity to the outside did not diminish the positivity inside.

This concept is especially important because the mass consciousness reckons that when you give something, it is lost to you, when you offer something, you are making a sacrifice, and the sacrifice always weakens or wearies you. But in my little meditation, nothing is lost, nothing is sacrificed, for if you activate and amplify the Power and Wisdom inside, you are dealing with a divine source without limits.

With joy, I imagined many little happy faces with each breath, and with love, little pink hearts. And when I was reminded that genuine love is always strong, I imagined a small but muscular arm holding the tiny hearts.

Could I actually *feel* these emotions I conjured up? Yes.

The technique was particularly effective in helping to resolve the fatiguing and dispiriting effects of a frightful period of sleeplessness in my life. At first it was a tentative assertion of my own Power, and tiny as it was, it helped me to believe in that Power and in myself.

Remember Aala's gift, Alma, and her conversations with her Father?

"Where is the Power and Wisdom, Father?" she once asked.

"In three parts – in your choices, decisions, and spirit mind; in the outer or intellectual part of you that makes the choice, in the inner or emotional part of you that makes the decision; and in your Spirit mind which enacts the unified choice and decision as a gift from Me."

"So I must fully agree with the choice?"

"Yes, or Spirit must wait till all parts of you *do* agree."

"Can I choose anything?"

"As long as it hurts no one, including yourself."

"As long as it is loving?"

"Yes."

"So I should let my Spirit Self choose for me?"

"Yes," said her Father. "You understand."

Love,

Anselam

Forgiveness

Dear Alma,

Your latest seems to summon the emotion of forgiveness . . . Larah is distressed over her fancied one who has not returned her affections, and you are dismayed over Arn who has ignored yours.

It is not difficult to believe that life, yours and mine, is sacred. And if so, there is, despite what we have been taught about our worth, a holiness about us. But that inner core of Light and Beauty can be hidden if we act out of keeping with it – if we live as if the sacredness does not exist. When we do that, we create a false self, and worse, we even believe this false self is real. It is folly, perhaps innocent folly, but acknowledging it is essential to forgiveness.

We made this self that did not know what it was, and in its ignorance it attacked others and the world. Had it known what it was, it would not have made that mistake. So we need to forgive its error, and that is not difficult – it simply did not know what it was, and while it lay in ignorance it lived an illusion.

Earlier in life, Alma, you studied *A Course in Miracles*, so recall what it says about forgiveness.

"What could you want forgiveness cannot give?" it asks. "Do you want peace? Forgiveness offers it. Do you want happiness, a quiet mind, a certainty of purpose, and a sense of worth and beauty that transcends the world? Do you want care and safety, and the warmth of sure protection always? Do you want a quietness that cannot be disturbed, a gentleness that can never be hurt, a deep abiding comfort, and a rest so perfect it can never be upset?

"All this forgiveness offers you, and more. It sparkles on your eyes as you awake, and gives you joy with which to meet the day. It soothes your forehead while you sleep, and rests upon your eyelids so you see no dreams of fear and evil, malice and attack. And when you wake again, it offers you another day of happiness and peace. All this forgiveness offers you and more."[51]

Love,

Anselam

Amish Forgiveness

Dear Alma and Larah,

Perhaps this will help.

Refuse to forgive and you must forever dwell in that grim land of slights and slanders, of bickering and brooding, of unresolved hurt and endless insult – a world of pain and punishment wherein you hold the sword of guilt to the throats of those who have offended you. Is this not a fearful world, completely devoid of tenderness and compassion?

Refusal to forgive is a mechanism of separation. In *The URANTIA Book* Christ tells Peter and James: "When a wise man understands the inner impulses of his fellows, he will love them. And when you love your brother you have already forgiven him. The child, being immature and lacking the fuller understanding of the depth of the child-father relationship, must frequently feel a sense of guilty separation from a father's full approval, but the true father [or true mother] is never conscious of such separation."[52]

In autumn 2006, Charles Roberts, a quiet milkman, went mad and shot ten young girls in an Amish school in Pennsylvania, killing five, and then himself. When Roberts, thirty-two, was buried behind the small Methodist church not far from the one-room school house he had desecrated, his wife Marie and their three small children stood shattered at the gravesite. Probably half of the seventy-five mourners were Amish.

Days earlier, Amish emissaries had visited Marie and invited her to the funeral of one of the slain girls. At the urging of Amish leaders, a fund was created for Roberts' widow and her fatherless children.

"It's the love, the forgiveness, the heartfelt forgiveness they have toward the family," said a chaplain who came all the way from Colorado to help. "I broke down and cried seeing it displayed."[53]

To Forgiveness,

Anselam

Expelling Dire Consequences

Dear Arn,

When you have done something wrong, you ask, how do the consequences of the wrong, the pain caused to yourself and another, disappear?

"The truth is that when you ask forgiveness you hope that the dire consequences of what you have done will be wiped away," said the Mother. "But that is possible only if the causes of the error you have committed have themselves disappeared. If you have made a mistake through ignorance, the ignorance must disappear. If you have made a mistake through bad will, the bad will must disappear and be replaced by goodwill. Mere regret will not do, it must be accompanied by a step forward.

"For the universe is constantly evolving; nothing is at a standstill.

"Therefore it is not a vague and abstract forgiveness that one should ask of the Divine, but the power to make the necessary progress. For only an inner transformation can wipe out the consequences of the act."[54]

A person who has abused a very young child due to a perverted addiction will never escape the ravages of guilt, that is, the consequence of his abuse, until he has expelled the addiction. Only a new man can forgive the old – because the old still wants to abuse. You cannot forgive yourself for something you still want to do.

Ask for a higher understanding, and a lower impulse will disappear.

With Affection,

Anselam

The Higher Morality of the Power and Wisdom

Dear Arn,

You are right – the transformed man can forgive himself because *kindness* has transformed him, kindness has stopped his lament, his repining and self-blame. He is marked now by self-control governed by love, self-appreciation imbued with clemency, a demeanor suffused with grace, an outward look lit by approval, geniality, and generosity. He is no longer the man who betrayed a trust, who debased a child, disparaged a mate, or defrauded a partner . . . He is *trustworthy*. He is his higher self in action.

He is the Abraham Lincoln in this story:

During the Civil War, Robert E. Lee' s two sons were captured by Northerners, one while wounded, and the other under a flag of truce offering to exchange himself for his disabled brother. In reprisal for the pending hanging of two union men, Secretary of War Stanton sought to hang the two Lee boys. Rushing to Richmond, General Lee implored Confederate President Jefferson Davis to intervene with Lincoln. "You need not worry," Davis said, "because Abraham Lincoln will not permit such an outrage."

"Stanton will carry out this diabolical purpose," answered Lee, "and Lincoln will know nothing about it."

So Davis telegraphed Lincoln.

Nearing midnight, Stanton entered the White House, answering an obligatory call from the president. Waving the telegram, Lincoln asked, "What does this mean?"

"Mr. President, the lives of those two Union captains are as precious to their families as are the lives of those Lee boys to their family," Stanton answered. "If our men are hanged in Richmond, both sons of Robert E. Lee should be hanged."

"Stanton, we are not savages," said Lincoln. "Let us see what the Book says." And opening the Bible, he stated: "Stanton, here is a command from Almighty God: 'Vengeance is mine; I will repay, saith the Lord.'"

Judgment was God's prerogative, not man's.

Lincoln then telegraphed the commandant of Fortress Monroe: "Immediately release both of the sons of Robert E. Lee and send them back to their father. Abraham Lincoln."[55]

To Love,

Anselam

Immediately release both of the sons of Robert E. Lee and send them back to their father.

Abraham Lincoln

Prefer the Meaning that Elevates

Dear Arn and Alma,

A difficult question: Is there a principal advisement of the higher self? A main message?

Try this.

"Prefer the meaning that elevates and you will always be right," Sai Baba told the Academy in 1962.[56] Or, the interpretation that inspires is the truth.

So, when a person undergoes difficulty, what does the difficulty mean, how do you interpret it? If the interpretation is purely negative, purely painful, purely self-belittling, it is not the right interpretation, because those imposed meanings do not elevate and do not inspire. (You know, "*I'm a victim!*" you sob. "*People did me wrong!*" you moan. "*I'm repulsive!*" you sigh. Did any of these interpretations uplift you, buoy you?)

If you say, "that experience was the worst of my life; it was nothing but humiliation and suffering, and as a result I think less of myself, in fact, I wonder if I deserve anything" – if you say *that* is the meaning of the experience, you are cast down, nullified, neutered, you are worthless and treated as worthless; if you say you have nothing but anger for what happened, or nothing but regret, if you say all these things, where have you elevated yourself, or inspired yourself? And whenever you have done neither, your interpretation is *wrong*. You have the meaning of the experience *wrong*. That's the marrow of the statement: "Prefer the meaning that elevates and you will always be right."

So you have to change your mind. The past can inspire if you construe it *as the past*; it is *not* the present, it is *not* you now. People who become their spiritual essence are like the sea – always throwing out onto the shore the flotsam and jetsam, the crud and the defilement, the impurity and the false interpretations afloat, so that they can be what they really are – pure spirit, beauty, love.

Every single human experience is a reminder either that you are living that pure reality or that you are about to – both of which are elevating thoughts.

"Prefer the meaning that elevates, and you will always be right," says Baba. That, I think, is the main message of the higher self.

In Friendship,

Anselam

P.S. I promise to tell you about Lord Dakshinamurty and the Sea.

Good News

Dear Arn,

An example of preferring the meaning that elevates?

Roberto De Vincenzo, a great Argentine golfer when I was young, once won a championship, and with cheque in hand walked into the parking lot. There a teary, young woman rushed up, commended his play, and told a frightening story of her little son, gravely ill. Penniless, she could no longer pay for doctors or medicine and knew not where to turn.

Deeply moved, Roberto endorsed his cheque over to her, saying, "Make some good days for the baby."

Later, at lunch, a Professional Golf Association dignitary reminded De Vincenzo of the woman.

"I have news for you," he said. "She's a phony. She has no sick baby. She's not even married. She fleeced you, my friend."

"You mean there is no baby who is dying?" muttered Roberto.

"Right."

"That's the best news I've heard all week," said Roberto.[57]

Cheers,

Anselam

A Young Apostate

Dear Alma,

I used to think I understood the simple statements of the Masters, but again and again, my understanding lacked application.

How does – "prefer the meaning that elevates and you will always be right" – apply to your young apostate? You have a precocious student who even in grade 6 has rejected religious teachings of your school. His parents are of similar mind, though the student agrees not with all they say either.

My advice?

Anthony De Mello told of an anxious couple who complained to the Master that their son had rejected the religion of his forefathers and declared himself "a freethinker."

Said the Master, "Not to worry. If the lad is really thinking for himself, the Mighty Wind is bound to arise that will carry him to the place where he belongs."[58]

Love,

Anselam

Deers and Dogs

Dear Arn,

Yes, put wisdom into practice, or it is useless.

"Once the deers of the forest gathered in a great assembly and discussed their own cowardice in the face of the pursuing hounds," Baba related. "They argued, 'Why should we, who are equipped with fleeter feet and sharp antlers be afraid of these insignificant dogs?' At last, a resolution was moved and passed that no deer should henceforth flee before hounds, but even while the cheering was going on, they heard the distant baying of the hounds, and not one stayed there; all . . . fled as fast as their legs could carry them! The resolution could not be put into practice!"[59]

. . . I no sooner sent this story, Arn, than received your humorous reply . . . Fed up with dictation from above and afar, your teachers in a professional development frenzy voted to dump the kowtowing to central office, the endless accountability, all the government tests, new certification requirements and new duties. Yes, I heard it too in my time, and said it too – let us go our own way, let us believe in ourselves, let us assert that superb teachers will create superb curricula . . . No sooner said than your teachers heard the baying of the hounds among the parents, demanding proof their children were advancing according to proper standards, then they heard the school board demanding these same standards, then they heard the government insisting on them, and then they fell silently in line. Their resolutions could not be put into practice.

There are applications of the story. People resolve to be more loving, to listen better, to cast off doubt, cynicism, negativity, prejudice, procrastination, anger, addictions, attachments, attack, self-disparagement, suffering, bad habits, bad thought, bad talk. They resolve to become self-reliant, even self-realized.

Make no mistake: such resolutions are necessary. But they are often resolutions wherein the mind, as presently conceived, is badly compromised. You cannot easily expect yourself to remove one vice when you are afflicted by several other related vices. If you say, "I remove my doubts," but keep a prejudice that strongly questions the capabilities of a certain race or religion; or if you say, "I shall no longer procrastinate," but keep a prejudice that strongly doubts your own ability; or if you say, "I give up my castigation of others," but keep a delight in castigating them – if you make such resolutions, each with a reservation, the reservations will become the hounds in Baba's story.

In a related vein, how will the deer face the wolves without a different conception of themselves? How will you create a new world *for* yourself without a different conception *of* yourself? How will you face your troubles without changing your mind about the power of trouble? How will you become enlightened without jettisoning what you are not, and accepting what you are? How will you accept what you are without accepting a richer vision of what you think you are? How will you be strong by believing you are weak? How will you be determined by thinking that determination doesn't matter after all, in a world where determination is ever quelled?

"I am never satisfied with the declaration of intentions!" Baba declared. "I must taste the *Ananda* [bliss] of putting them into action! I express my Love through every act, every intention of mine. More than floods of eloquence in praise of that intention and millions of words written in elaboration of the theme, I insist, by my own example, on immediate and complete fulfillment."[60]

No equivocation, no false starts. Each intention must be consummated in action.

How is it possible? Baba would say, because I know the Power that I am, and I have accepted that Power completely.

To Action,

Anselam

J.M.W. Turner and Trust

Dear Arn,

Right, self-trust is the key to manifesting your intentions.

An example of self-trust in action?

Joseph Mallord William Turner (1775-1851) was a remarkable British painter of landscapes and seascapes, a creator of masterpieces of clear light and striking color, including "The Fighting Temeraire" and "Shipwreck of the Minotaur." One of his great works was of the fire that ravaged the British Houses of Parliament in 1834, a scene of immense drama and force. Hanging the painting very much unfinished, Turner had three hours to conclude it before the public were admitted to the gallery. Calmly, he added the necessary brush strokes, then he wheeled about and walked off without a single backward look. Seeing it all, the painter Daniel Maclise remarked, "There, that's masterly; he does not stop to look at his work; he *knows* it is done and he is off."[61]

That is self-trust, Arn, no second thoughts, no hesitation.

To Self-confidence,

Anselam

More Self-Trust

Dear Alma,

Yes, declare with sureness, "my marriage is refreshed and revitalized; my mood is confident and constructive; my teaching is inspired; my parenthood, upbearing." All the Power and Wisdom of your Spirit Self will materialize these determinations.

Often, Master Baba told my friend and mentor Larry Wayne, "Use the Power, Larry, use the Power!"

Yes, use it, Alma, trust it, be it.

Fondly,

Anselam

P.S. I quoted Larry Wayne and his partner Grace Johnston once before. The heart of their teaching is that the Power and Wisdom resides in each person; i.e., each one *is* the Power and Wisdom, or Spirit. To unite with your power is the purpose of life. Grace has long conversed directly with Spirit, and the answers to her many questions brought in time hundreds of pages of insight and instruction, the foundation of an entire approach to self-realization that she and Larry took deeper and deeper.[62] It profoundly uplifted me.

May I share some of it in future?

Acceptance

Dear Alma and Arn,

In order for self-trust to operate, you must *accept* the Self you trust; you must *accept* yourself as totally trustworthy. Like all simple sentences of truth, this means much more than you think. You must believe in yourself as the source of your own happiness, your own joy, your own fulfillment, as the solution to any problem, the inspiration for any endeavor. Perhaps a way to understand this is to write down all those things you do not trust yourself to be, do or understand, and then tell yourself that real self-trust would create this being, doing, understanding, and that acceptance is knowing that you are a Spirit of unlimited ability and boundless worth, who is the living proof of those qualities. This is no picayune belief; it is utterly encompassing

Why is acceptance of what we are so difficult?

People will not accept what they are because the truth is constellations beyond what they believe they are. But that must be so if they are, as Master Maharaj told us, "*the infinite potentiality, the inexhaustible possibility.*"[63]

We are not saying to a .294 hitter in baseball, "you are really a .300 hitter"; that he might accept because it is a jot from where he is now. We are saying something much more.

"In silence and true humility, I seek God's glory, to behold it in the Son Whom He Created as my Self," said Jesus in *A Course in Miracles*.[64] "God is with me . . . He covers me with kindness and with care, and holds in love the

Son He shines upon, who also shines on Him."[65] And this statement, Arn and Alma: "My true identity is so secure, so lofty, sinless, glorious and great, wholly beneficent and free from guilt, that Heaven looks to it to give it light."[66]

If you cannot accept these declarations, you see how difficult it is to accept what you are.

To Acceptance,

Anselam

Lightheartedness

Dear Arn,

The Masters always warned against taking things too seriously. One told this story about himself.

"My very first disciple was so weak that the exercises killed him. My second disciple drove himself crazy from his earnest practice of the exercises I gave him. My third disciple dulled his intellect through too much contemplation. But the fourth managed to keep his sanity."

"How?" someone asked.

"Possibly because he was the only one who refused to do the exercises."[67]

To Buoyancy,

Anselam

Steady Application

Dear Alma and Arn,

Allowing humor, let's not end this portion *too lightly.*

"Be steady in *Sadhana* [spiritual practice] and never hesitate once you have decided on it," said Baba. "When the bus is moving on, the dust will be floating behind as a cloud: it is only when it stops with a jerk that the dust will envelop the faces of the passengers. So, keep moving, keep steadily engaged in *Sadhana.* Then, the cloudy dust of the objective world will not cover your face."[68]

Yes, a continuous movement forward, undivided, uninterrupted . . . lest you forget who you are.

Repeat one of the myriad names of the Lord, regularly, Baba urged, so as to remember your high calling. The name should be your last thought in this life.

"There was a shop-keeper once who . . . decided to remember the Name with his last breath, by a short cut; he named his sons after the various Avatars, for he knew that he was bound to call them when he was about to die," related Baba. "The moment came at last and as expected, he called on his sons by name, one by one. There were six of them, and so he called the Lord by proxy six times in all. The boys came and stood round his cot and as he surveyed the group the thought that came to the dying man's mind just as he was about to die was, 'Alas, they have all come away; who will look after *the shop* now?' You see, his shop was his very breath all through life and he could not switch it on to God at short notice."[69]

Without rigorous discipline of mind, the world turns you into itself and away from your essence. So habitual must the focus on yourself as Spirit be, that you are not even aware you are acting as the Power and Wisdom.

"Let the mountains fall; let the sea overwhelm the land, but do not give up your *Sadhana*," warned Baba.[70]

To Practice,

Anselam

Is God Necessary?

Dear Alma and Arn,

Alma, you ask a very important question – Does self-realization require God?

The word "God" matters not as much as you think it does.

You could pray to "Fullness" or "Completeness," or "Allness" or "Light" or "Spirit." You could long to be full or complete, aware of All, a lantern for All, or a Great Spirit for yourself. You could see the distant reaches of your potential as the "Power and Wisdom" or the effulgence of your own soul as the "Presence." You could call your highest conception of Self, Splendor, or Divine Splendor. You could call the gifts of the spirit *Siddhis*, or you could just call them cloudless sight, unclogged hearing, subtler feeling, deeper understanding. Words are just symbols. But perhaps the word "more" is the key – more abundance, more wisdom, more love, more sincerity, serenity, Spirit, acceptance, reverence, trust. More of who and what you are, always more, plumbless, fathomless . . . You are about to emerge from a chrysalis across chasms and corridors and eons until the embryo that was you becomes a Master of the Deep. Call your destiny whatever, but never forget its grandeur.

To More,

Anselam

Desisting

Lord Dakshinamurthy and the Ocean

Dear Alma and Arn,

Did the Masters craft an image of the process of self-realization?

Yes.

Baba often spoke of Lord Dakshinamurty, the divine teacher of spiritual wisdom, who once strolled slowly along the sea-beach, meditating: "He turned towards the waves and watched the unending succession of breakers. He saw a dry little twig on the crest of a wave in the distance; it was being passed on from one wave to another, from trough to crest, from crest to trough, until it was cast on the sands on the shore, near where He stood! Dakshinamurty was astounded at the egoism of the Ocean that would not give asylum to even a tiny twig. Sensing His reaction, the Ocean declared, in words that He could understand, 'Mine is neither egoism nor anger; it is only the duty of self-preservation. I should not allow the slightest blot to deface my grandeur. If I allow this twig to mar my splendour, it will be the first step in my downfall.'"[1]

Misdeeds, misconceptions, scum, sullage, impurities, must be cast off so the Sea is its unspoiled, pristine Self.

What would you discard?

I have asked Larah too.

To Dakshinamurty,

Anselam

How Not to Evolve

Dear Alma and Arn,

Good, you have thought of what is not useful to you.

One day after Aala had become a great teacher, a student asked a strange question.

"Aala, what is the easiest way *not* to reach self-realization, *not* to be the Power and Wisdom?" Now, the student merely wanted to understand better what she *thought* she understood.

"Do not love yourself," Aala answered. "Be short-tempered with your thoughts, your efforts, ignore your body, discredit your mind, be hard on yourself, treat yourself as a nonentity. Punish yourself for your mistakes, and remind yourself of them often so you can punish yourself again and again. If an error be worth fifty lashes, remember it ten times for 500 lashes, or better, one hundred times for 5000 lashes. Some people have flogged themselves a hundred thousand times for the same fault or frailty. Generate self-anger, self-belittlement. And don't forgive yourself, for that would stop the whipping. Become a workaholic, don't rest, don't take a holiday, don't treat yourself, don't comfort yourself, work instead, think of others instead, focus on what needs correction in *their* minds. Examine *their* thoughts, never your own, spend no time on yourself, especially on how to grow, to improve, to see more clearly. Leave yourself out, sacrifice yourself, ignore yourself, neglect yourself, discount yourself. Look at others, never yourself."

"Isn't thinking of yourself first selfish?" the student asked an old question.

"It can be," said Aala. "But not if its purpose is to make you more aware, to help you grow in spirit. Really, the greatest help you can be is to grow in spirit, but you must grow first or your help is limited. If you rush into the world attempting to rescue it and are immature, what effect will you have? If you are no better off in spirit than those you would save, how will you save them? If you have thought little or never about your own evolution, how can you help others to evolve?"

Over and over when Masters Larry Wayne and Grace Johnston ask students for their highest goal, their life purpose, they say things like "helping others," "serving humanity," "uplifting society," "saving the afflicted," – all admirable enough as the mass consciousness reckons, but rather like wanting to do heart surgery before learning incisions . . . or implying that your conscience should be everyone else's guide . . . You who would be your brother's keeper, have you asked him what he wants, Alma? If he says, "nothing," will you tell him what he *should* want, Arn? And if he says something, will you weaken him by doing it for him? No wonder Maharaj said that anyone who thinks he knows what is good for others is dangerous.[2]

All these aspirations are other-focused, part of a mass consciousness that would have you sacrifice yourself. Concentrating on the outside permits you to ignore, even repress, your duty to yourself. The ego would have you do anything, from hurting others to helping them, as long as you are so absorbed in them that you don't look into yourself, the only place where genuine peace and fulfillment reside. Thus, the fixation outside of yourself is a form of irresponsibility to yourself, a delaying, a covering up, a respectable way of being *disrespectful to yourself.*

Love,

Anselam

How You Hurt Yourself

Dear Arn,

You asked how you can hurt yourself.

In general, by denying all that you are.

By ignoring your passion, your health and happiness, by refusing harmony and peace, by scorning enthusiasm, intimacy and laughter, by pooh poohing inspiration, wonder and wisdom, by disbelieving in magic and miracles, perfection and enlightenment,

By cultivating regret and remorse, by second-guessing your choices and agonizing over the results, by doubting yourself, disparaging yourself, by fixing on how things go wrong and by obsessing over the fetid fruits of failure.

By canceling holidays, abandoning celebrations, by being too serious, too stern.

By not going to shows, to musicals, to parties, to games, to exhibits, to the mountains, to the lake, to the sea, by not playing.

By believing you are undeserving and unforgivable, innately sinful and cast from God, by condemning yourself, by being negative, weak, angry, inefficient, irresolute and insincere.

By disparaging your imagination, your creativity, by limiting your horizons, your potential, by refusing to expand your interests, refusing to grow, by declaring all that you are not interested in, and by re-declaring it every time you encounter it, as if it were a mark of identity, a badge of your shrunken status.

By blaming others for your failures, by asserting your impotence.

By reveling in disasters and tragedies, and, surprise! surprise! by being *depressed.*

By being unkind and unwelcoming

By being a coward.

By sacrificing yourself for others (yes, this too), by thinking only of others, never yourself, never your mission, your purpose, your fulfillment, always theirs; by denying yourself joy, even hearty pleasure, by disloyalty to self, by never making a commitment to self, never standing tall, never trusting self.

And, worst of all sacrifices, by withholding love for *yourself.*

I always remember Larry's statement:

"Lack, unhappiness, pain, unreachable goals are all the mental crimes you commit against yourself. In a dream I heard the judge saying – 'And who is responsible for this crime?' Then, I heard myself reply – 'I am.' It is imperative to recognize, acknowledge and release this negative, destructive pattern, so you may be one with your potential and power."

You are an athlete, Arn, and there are special self-tortures for athletes too. When I was playing that strange Canadian winter game of curling, at which I reached a fairly decent competence, I kept a list of all the great shots I ever missed, and I rehearsed them regularly, as if memorizing a tragic poem, reliving the shock and deflation of defeat, wringing my hands, years and years later, over what might have been, if only I had done this instead of *that.* And in my little black book I would underscore the error again and again. Never forget this, I told myself harshly, angrily. Furious with the ineptitude, the foolishness of the shot, I was my own hyper-critical coach, brow-beating, bullying, bludgeoning *me.* The pressure I put on myself was unbearable, and I learned the ways to fail, and my idea of surprise was a new way to lose a championship at the last possible moment, rather like a hailstorm on harvest day, or a mother grizzly at the end of a lovely hike. Probably no one else in the country knew the negative aspect of the game as well. None could see as subtly all the tracks to discomfiture, even the faintest and most improbable, and I actually took pride in being able to foresee disaster, though it was a weird sort of pride when it was my own disaster. As I think now, it was a distorted delight in devastation; after all, I had predicted it. But while I took defeat graciously, I did not take it lightly. The postmortem lasted longer than the game, and I was not tender with myself – I was the sergeant and the greenhorn in my own boot camp. No wonder the sport exhausted me ... And even as I struggled to recover from my insomnia (mentioned earlier), and slept fitfully and fleetingly, a bad game or a bad call, though I was decades past my competitive years, could keep me up for another night.

What nonsense was this!

Now you need to understand some things here, Arn. This harshness against the self was *revealed* in the game of curling, but it was far deeper than the game; in fact, it was a way of being with myself that branched pervasively and dangerously into what I thought I was and how I must react. And always there was this brutal censor. Whenever something went wrong, whenever I was criticized, whenever I made bad choices, this egoistic autocrat held court. Anything that did not go well was the subject of endless internal interrogation, conducted by this censor that second-guessed everything and lauded nothing.

Almost incomprehensibly, these indignities against the self can seem so natural that they go unnoticed by our conscious minds. Others can often see them, but we have hidden them from ourselves. That was the case with me.

I sense from your latest, Arn, that your own censor is troubling you.

To the End of Censors,

Anselam

The Disturbance

Dear Alma and Arn,

Self-abuse is one of enlightenment's worst obstructions. You can hide it only so long before it must face the light, be acknowledged, forgiven, and cast onto Dakshinamurty's shore.

How did mine come out of hiding?

Suddenly I couldn't sleep. It was two or three days into a two-week summer course I was teaching on the Spirituality of Inspired Leadership. The course was meant to offer the highest teachings, and from those insights a feeling of love, encouragement and ultimately peace. And here I was feeling disturbed. It was agonizing, and I did not understand it, but the sleeplessness went away after the course, and things returned to normal.

It happened again the next summer when I did the course, and the summer after that. First it was perplexing, then annoying, then frightening. In the third summer, I left on holiday to the Okanagan Valley of British Columbia after the course, and in that ten days I slept like a baby, and assumed all was right again.

I returned home on August 4, and then for the first time when I was not teaching the course, it began again. I was now awake every hour of the night, I became despondent, I lost appetite, vitality and weight.

The remedy almost never came, likely because I resisted it. Perhaps as it was so simple, my academic mind would not accept it at first, and there were other problems with that mindset, as we shall see.

“You are on the edge of coming into your own Power,” Larry told me. “You need to accept it, claim it as your own. You need to stand for the reality you want to create, and then create it.”

“If I could only sleep, I could come into that Power,” I replied.

“No, you must come into the Power first, then you will sleep.”

I heard him, but I did not know what he meant . . .

So instead of turning to what I was, I focused on the disturbance and tried remedy after remedy, doubting them all and slipping perilously into a benumbed state of powerlessness.

The insomnia lasted until late February the next year.

In Truth,

Anselam

Direct Intervention

Dear Arn,

Your conjecture is plausible – the insomnia was caused by my unwitting harshness toward self, almost as if I had so driven a part of me to distraction by criticism, that that part could no longer sleep, had to be awake and vigilant all night long to avoid yet another criticism. There is something in what you say.

But there was a bigger issue underlying even that, and it was the issue of my own evolution. If this were how I would see the world and treat myself, my growth was stifled. I had to love myself more, be kinder to myself, more patient with self . . .

How did I survive sleeplessness for more than six months?

I was then attending classes of the Academy in Calgary, Alberta, under the guidance of Masters Wayne and Johnston. At one very crucial moment in my insomnia, Dr. Cruppe spoke to the class, and when he came to me, he fired a four barreled shot-gun, and each of the two hundred painful pieces of buckshot in my hide screamed the same – you have been unbelievably hard on yourself, impatient with self, brutal with self, serious with self, kinder by far to others than to self. Cruppe was only telling the truth, but it was devastating. Stroke for stroke, he stated what I was doing to myself; on and on it went. He knew if he did not set me straight, I could not survive. If I were to complete my life purpose, I had gone beyond when I could come to my senses without direct intervention. Someone in authority, a Master of the Academy, had to tell me what I would not tell myself.

When the good doctor finished, another Master, Dr. Elsa Lund, consoled me with the kind and loving word I had denied to myself.

That evening, my recovery slowly began.

Love,

Anselam

P.S. I also sent a letter to Master Sathya Sai Baba in India placing the disturbance in his hands, which was akin to placing it in the hands of what Larry and Grace call the Power and Wisdom.

Ending Self-Punishment

Dear Arn,

Strange how slowly some things come to light . . .

Sharing intimate details of your relationship with Alma is difficult, but your insights give hope.

You have long been just tolerating each other, civil but sniping, together but barely. Sexual intimacy has disappeared. You have wilted with inadequacy and impotence, and, frustratingly, it smacks of self-punishment. In your marriage, you have seen your mate primarily as a sexual object, something she warned you of years ago, something you dismissed. This diminishment of value hurt her, and knowing that you acted unlovingly, you feel callous and counterfeit – two stormy petrels of self-torment.

Self-punishment is usually directed symbolically and literally to the part of you that best represents the error made, the initial hurt. So you have taken from yourself the only thing you mistakenly valued in your partner. What better punishment or justice for one who has overemphasized sex than to remove sex altogether!

Self-love is called for, Arn . . . If you love Alma, you will not hurt her, because hurt creates guilt, and guilt demands punishment, and punishment extracts suffering – but the suffering originates from self-disgust or self-neglect . . . never self-love. Anyone who loves himself will never hurt another, because he knows *that* will hurt him. And he won't pain himself, if he truly respects himself.

So what to do?

Forgive yourself for underprizing Alma and for unfitting yourself.

Then go to her and start loving the whole girl.

Warmly,

Anselam

Escaping the Past

Dear Arn,

Like me, you are an historian, and all historians value the past as if it were their own soul and sustenance, and in many ways it is so.

But at some point one needs to escape the past.

Perhaps Aurobindo meant this when he said that only those maxims are true where their opposite was also true . . . So history has to be grasped but also released, it can lighten but also suppress, it can lend insight but also prevent growth. It has great value *and* great cost. Likewise, the patterns of our own past can be both helpful and unhelpful, helpful in providing familiarity and order, unhelpful in resisting anything untried. A pattern provides a groove of experience, and the marble rolls down the groove smoothly enough, but it knows only the groove, nothing new.

The construction of a new life is like the building of a new village. Once the village is conceived, it defines itself – the landscape is set, pathways are set, the shape is set. After the surveying and the platting, the subdivisions impose themselves along with avenues and streets and drives that become the only ways around and through, as private fences, lawns and gardens barricade and block alternate, often more direct routes. In a sense, the past of every village and every person has determined the present. If the mind of an individual could be mapped, it would look like a townsite, and however beautiful or elegant, drab or run down, it would be incredibly *fixed*. These are the ways we live and move and die, and the past has determined it all.

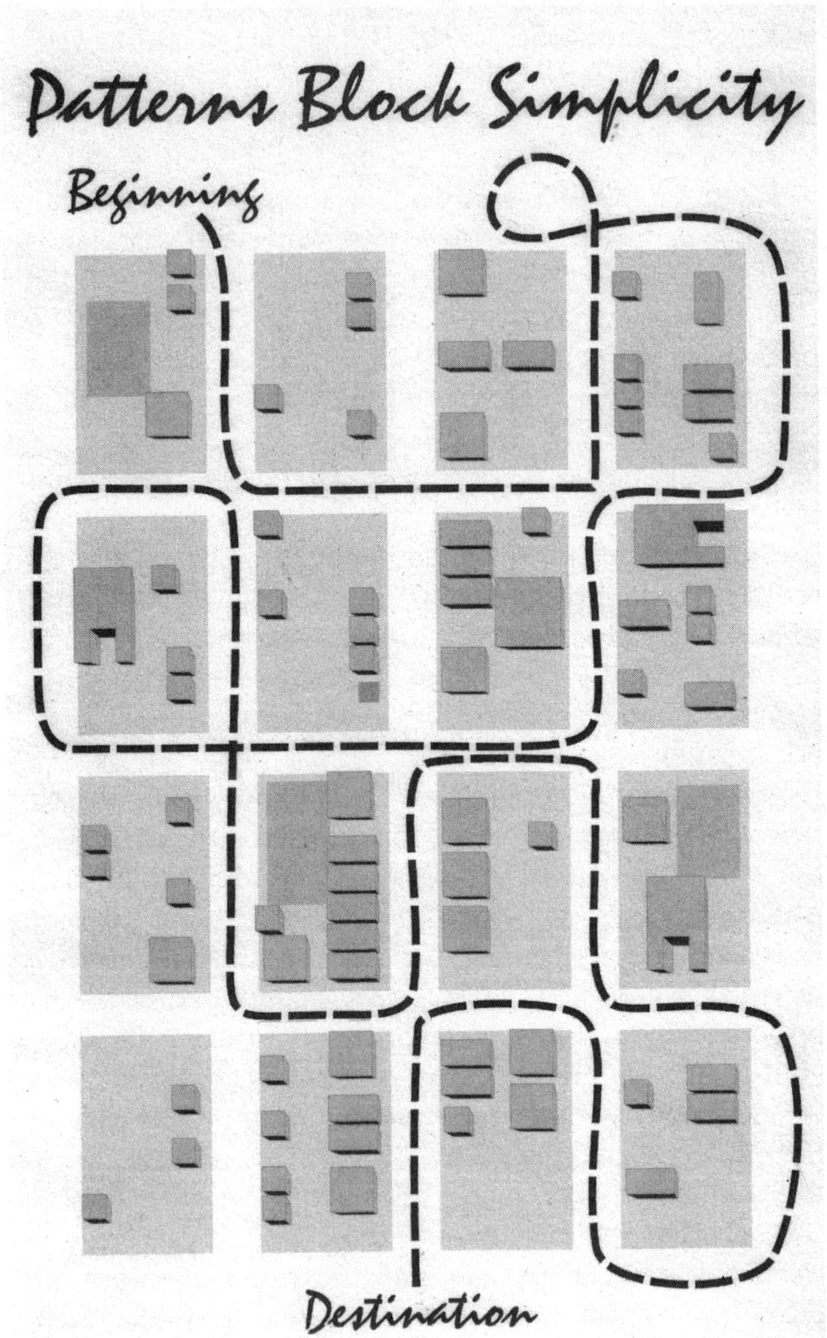

Patterns Block Simplicity

Beginning

Destination

People see the patterns they have created and accepted, they see what their conditioning has led them to see, they see what they have been taught to train their eyes on. As a young man, the English poet Alfred Lord Tennyson, suffered terribly from piles, so he went to a famous proctologist to ease his pain. Years later, after he became poet of the realm, he experienced a relapse and sought out the same proctologist for relief. Expecting now to be recognized, Tennyson was first disappointed, but when he bent over, the good doctor exclaimed, "Ah, Tennyson!"[3]

Patterns . . . I suppose a hemorrhoid can be as individual as a face, and that one can recognize a patient in a pile, but it is an awkward form of salutation, a cumbersome pattern. In the end, all patterns are cumbersome because they override other, often simpler ways of seeing, and sometimes they prevent the *very simplest way* of seeing a person – by looking at the face and remembering a name.

The Sufi Master Nasrudin was a smuggler, an admitted smuggler, who crossed the border with his donkey regularly. And regularly he was searched by border guards who sifted through the straw in the panniers on the donkey, sometimes burning the straw or steeping it in water. Never did the border guards find anything, though they grew increasingly annoyed at the obvious waxing prosperity of Nasrudin. After Nasrudin retired in opulence in another country, one of the customs agents approached him.

"You can tell me now, Nasrudin, whatever was it you were smuggling when we could never catch you out?"

"jjDonkeys," said Nasrudin.[4]

The border guards had trained their eyes on what Nasrudin was carrying, so they did not see what was carrying *him*. The past had conditioned their vision, blinkered it.

So it is with everyone's past.

Love,

Anselam

Past to Present

Dear Alma,

Oh, yes, Larry and Grace were very aware of the way the past thrust itself upon the present, like weeds invading a garden. I think it safe to say that everyone who ever came to them came with a troubled past, some with a nostalgic longing for a different past, others with an irrepressible wish to resolve hurt in the past. All were trapped in a bog of constraining conceptions about themselves.

Sri Yukteswar, Yogananda's teacher, sometimes encountered students who wondered about their own worth, and he would tell them: "Forget the past. The vanished lives of all men are dark with many shames. Human conduct is ever unreliable until man is anchored in the Divine."[5]

"One has continually to leave behind his past lives," said Aurobindo. "If one keeps an exaggerated feeling for an inferior past it must make it more difficult to develop the entire person for a higher future . . . Retrospection is seldom healthy as it turns one towards a past consciousness."[6]

"Don't go into the past," Larry told me. "There is no value in that. The negative ego is always trying to fix something in the past when you should be in the active present."

It is a curious blend of forgetfulness and transcendence that Masters of the deep practice. Referring to himself, as if distancing himself from the events, Krishnamurti once said, "He doesn't remember his childhood, the schools and the caning. He was told later by the very teacher who hurt him that he used to cane him practically every day;

he would cry and be put out on the verandah until the school closed and the teacher would come out and ask him to go home, otherwise he would still be on the verandah. He was caned, this man said, because he couldn't study or remember anything he had read or been told. Later the teacher couldn't believe that that boy was the man who had given the talk he had heard. He was greatly surprised and unnecessarily respectful. All those years passed without leaving scars, memories, on his mind; his friendships, his affections, even those years with those who had ill-treated him – somehow none of these events, friendly or brutal, have left marks on him. In recent years a writer asked if he could recall all those rather strange events and happenings, and when he replied that he could not remember them and could only repeat what others had told him, the man openly, with a sneer, stated that he was putting it on and pretending. He never consciously blocked any happening, pleasant or unpleasant, entering into his mind. They came, leaving no mark, and passed away."[7]

In some form, Krishnamurti had transcended memory itself, or perhaps it was the pain of memory.

Tagore, too, knew how memory could imprison one in the past by reliving experiences over and over, without rest or resolution. And he knew the great value we accorded memory as well as how the mind so often drained vitality by interfering with the here and now. Said he, "Memory, the priestess, kills the present and offers its heart to the shrine of the dead past."[8] But only the present was real. "Do not say, 'It is morning,' and dismiss it with a name of yesterday," Tagore wrote. "See it for the first time as a newborn child that has no name."[9] Yes, the engaging present, the cure for the discouraging past – "His own mornings are new surprises to God," the Master added.[10]

We often have it wrong, Larry said. "We remember the past and forget the present, when it should be the other way round."

To the Present,

Anselam

Basking in the Present Process

Dear Arn,

"I wonder if some of you have noticed you are forgetting things?" Larry asked one class. "Now you need to know what is happening here. When you forget what you are doing, you are not in the moment, and when you are not in the moment, you are not in control of your life. You are doing things, but your mind is elsewhere, so you are not getting the most out of what you are doing or enjoying it, or seeing, feeling, experiencing the spirit part of it." How can what you are doing be enjoyable, worthy, or expanding if you are not focused on it? How can it evolve or grow if you are not in the picture?" How can you appreciate the moment if you are absent?

To be out of the moment is like watching a miniature TV screen in your car while you are driving. Or asking directions, then not listening to them, or hearing part of a joke, then missing the punch line. It is like forfeiting the camaraderie with friends by thinking of yesterday or tomorrow, someone else or some other place, or relinquishing the joy of sex by replaying an insult at dinner, or by recalling a task neglected at noon, when you were equally absent.

Fulton Oursler used to say, "we crucify ourselves between two thieves: regret for yesterday and fear of tomorrow."[11]

What is needed is the discipline to go with the flow, to discard extraneous thoughts, to move easily and lightly to each new enterprise, and to be the master of that experience. You automatically remove yourself from the Power whenever you are not taking control of NOW.

So, tomorrow and the next day, observe yourself carefully and reset your thoughts on what you are being and doing whenever you wander. *Ask for discipline, the discipline of your own mind.* Live more, much more in the present. Congratulate yourself when you do, berate yourself not, when you don't. Forgive lapses, however oft, and return to the NOW.

Remember that the moment is the scaffold from which you sculpt the image of what you will be, the edifice of yourself. Remove the scaffold, and you will never reach the heights. Instead, constantly build it, adding a new level with each new moment, staying, always staying on the task at hand, shaping it, moulding it, enhancing it, expanding it, making it more and more elegant and inspiring.

During my gradual recovery from insomnia, I journeyed up the Rideau Canal from Kingston to Ottawa, Canada, on a five-day river cruise that took two hours by bus. Aboard the *Kawartha Voyageur*, I could nap and sleep quite well – because I knew I was in the moment, in the process of gliding down life's river, silently, serenely. It was a piece of paradise, because I was reveling in the moment, cherishing the experience, *and not wanting to be anywhere else.*

To Basking,

Anselam

Escaping Separation

Dear Arn and Alma,

By all means, choose to be where you are, and want to be where you choose.

Anthony De Mello told of a Master who was banished from his native land for the "good" of the country, though perhaps for his own good too, for he who would tell the truth must have one foot in the stirrup, as the Turks used to say.

Did he ever feel nostalgia, his disciples asked.

"No," the Master said.

"But it is inhuman not to miss one's home," they insisted.

"You cease to be an exile when you discover that creation is your home," answered the Master.[12]

You create the reality of your home, so you are at home everywhere, and when you are in the Power and Wisdom there is an unmistakable feeling of *being at home* and of *being a creator.*

Love,

Anselam

Human Negative Need Prevents Self-Love

Dear Alma,

"What does human negative need have to do with self love?" you ask. Such need is doing something so that someone else will approve, living so that others are pleased. Yours is a very important question because it is difficult to explain convincingly why you must love yourself and what happens when you do.

Simply put, if you think you need someone else's validation you can't validate yourself, you can't *value* yourself, and without value you will not believe you deserve love. Condemnation perhaps, reformation certainly, but never love. You are lovable not because you have *some* value, but because you are priceless; said differently, you are lovable because you are love itself, and love loves itself. It does not have misgivings about itself . . .

If you tie yourself to the opinions of friends or colleagues, students or superiors, wanting their validation, you won't be able to love yourself for what you are, because you will be allowing their opinions to hurt you, and no one who permits such wounding can really be said to love herself. A self-loving soul is also a strong soul, who stands for what she is, stands for herself, completely alone, and refuses all thought word and deed that would make her weak. A self-loving soul is disciplined. I am not suggesting you shut your ears to criticism, but I *am* suggesting that you shut them to criticism you interpret as an axe blow to your self-esteem and self-worth. Criticism can redirect you, refine you, yes, but it can never fell you.

Now when you feel hurt and weak, you will be fear-ridden. And when you are fear-ridden, love is the farthest thing from your mind. A fearful person is full of misgiving and self-doubt. In that state, she will find it very, very difficult to love herself. Why? Because love is kindness, peace, and joy. Here she is not thinking of kindness; she is brooding on threat. She's not at peace; she's under attack. She's not joyous; she's worried. She has accepted a state of mind that is inherently frightening and disturbing, hence *unloving*. Love knows no threat, no conflict, no war, no anxiety.

So whenever you hand your self-worth over to someone else, someone else's opinion, you cannot love yourself. You put yourself at risk, and no one who loves herself will do that. You may be fully aware of the dangers of judgment, and you may even teach those dangers. But this also means that you must not be affected by anyone *who judges you*, because she knows not what she does. Your infinite value is always in place. This does not mean that a comment by someone could not make you even more loving. You see, your Spirit Self, will, in the gentlest way, offer many, many suggestions, all intended to make you more of who and what you are, that is, more and more loving. But it will never suggest that you depend on another's whim for your own precious value, because then your love of self would always be in jeopardy. The attachment to that whim would prevent you from loving yourself fully. So discard these attachments, devalue these judgments, drop this bondage, and then and only then can you love yourself. Freedom and love are ever partners.

Alma, human negative need is a false surrender to the opinions of others. And there is another false surrender – to your own ego.

Love,

Anselam

Arjuna and Krishna Dismounting the Chariot

Dear Arn,

You say you never surrender to the opinions of others, but that you occasionally surrender to the dictates of your ego. Well, that is a start. You admit to sharp exchanges between you and your principal, each of you insisting you are right. Your intellectualism slashes colleagues and rules Alma when you argue.

Having bent to your ego, how do you feel?

Recall that during the great Kurukshetra war between good and evil, Arjuna chose Krishna as his charioteer.

Arjuna, the supreme archer, was always proud to have Krishna as his "servant," and near the end of the conflict a dispute arose over who should dismount first from the chariot – Master Arjuna, or servant, Krishna – Arjuna protesting pridefully that as master he should dismount last. But Krishna insisted otherwise. After a long, pleading display, Arjuna unwillingly went first. Krishna then dismounted, and instantly the chariot burst afire! As Krishna explained later, the incendiary arrows and spears of the enemy were powerless as long as He was aboard, but the moment he left they exploded into flame.

Thus was Arjuna's pride humbled by his teacher.[13]

When you are one with the Power and Wisdom, you are omnipotent; when separate from it, you are vulnerable. Krishna represented the infinity of this Intelligence, Strength, and Protection that solves any problem. For many, Christ represents it; for others Buddha represents it.

The self-realized are constantly in touch with this inner majesty.

The ego thinks it can do without the majesty and power, without God, whom it would like to replace. The strong resistance to God is the ego talking. Not to hear the voice of God, said Aurobindo, "is the world's idea of sanity."[14] *Not to hear it!* The ego is Arjuna who wants to step off the chariot last, but without Krishna's protection, he would be burnt to a cinder.

So the ego has an inflated self-view, but it is also more than that, or perhaps better said, *less* than that.

To the Power,

Anselam

Self-Condemnation is also Egoism

Dear Alma,

You say you surrender too often to the opinions of others, but seldomly to your ego.

Others have better ideas, better delivery, and you are humbler than they are . . . Perhaps it would help to know more about the ego.

"Once, Krishna pretended to be suffering from head-ache, intense, unbearable head-ache," Baba told. "He acted that role quite . . . realistically . . . He wound warm clothes around His head, rolled restlessly in bed. His eyes were red and He was in evident distress. The face too appeared swollen and pale. Rukmini, Satyabhama and the other queens rushed about with all kinds of remedies and palliatives. But they were ineffective. At last, they consulted Narada and he went into the sick room to consult Krishna Himself and find out which drug would cure Him.

"Krishna directed him to bring – what do you think the drug was? – the dust of the feet of a true devotee! In a trice, Narada manifested himself in the presence of some celebrated devotees of the Lord; but, they were too humble to offer the dust of their feet to be used by their Lord as a drug!

"That is also a kind of egoism. 'I am low, mean, small, useless, poor, sinful, inferior' – such feelings also are egoistic; when the ego goes, you do not feel either superior or inferior. No one would give the dust wanted by the Lord; they were too worthless, they declared. Narada came back disappointed to the sickbed. Then, Krishna asked him,

'Did you try Brindavan where the Gopis live?'

The Gopis were cowherd girls, rural folk, uneducated, but they exemplified the richest, unconditional love for God. Their devotion was complete, unquestioning, given freely and joyously.

Continued Baba, "The Queens laughed at the suggestion and even Narada asked in dismay, 'What do they know of devotion?' Still, the sage had to hurry thither. When the Gopis heard Krishna was ill and that the dust of their feet might cure Him, without a second thought they shook the dust off their feet and filled his hands with the same. By the time Narada reached Dwaraka, the headache had gone. It was just a five-day drama, to teach that self-condemnation is also egoism . . ."[15]

Would Sanson, now eight, understand this story, Alma?

Love,

Anselam

"These Bloodless Pedants"

Dear Arn,

You are an intellectual, and I am one of sorts, too – so I know something about us.

May I speak of Masters of the Academy and their relationship with intellectuals? Because the Masters have access to all knowledge through their superconscious minds, or the Power and Wisdom within, they often surprise professors and scientists who speak to them with "precise insight into their specialized fields of knowledge," as Yogananda said of his teacher Yukteswar.[16] Scientist David Bohm experienced this with Krishnamurti, psychiatrist Samuel Sandweiss, with Sai Baba, and psychologists Helen Schucman, William Thetford, and Gerald Jampolsky, with Jesus of *A Course in Miracles*. Yukteswar read little save for the ancient Hindu scriptures, yet Yogananda said, "When he so desired Master could instantly attune himself to the mind of any man."[17]

There was a completeness about Masters that pedants lacked. One day a celebrated savant appeared at Yukteswar's ashram bent on impressing the Master. Said Yogananda who sat discreetly in the corner listening, "The rafters resounded as the guest recited passages from the *Mahabharata*, *Upanishads*, and *bhasyas* (commentaries) of Shankara."

When at last the pedant took breath, Yukteswar said simply, "I am waiting to hear you.

"Quotations there have been in superabundance. But what original commentary can you supply, from the uniqueness of your particular life? What holy text have you absorbed and made your own? In what ways have these timeless truths renovated your nature? Are you content to be a hollow victrola [record player] mechanically repeating the words of other men?"

Yogananda, nearby, could scarcely contain his mirth.

"I give up!" the scholar surrendered. "I have no inner realization."

"These bloodless pedants smell unduly of the lamp," Yukteswar commented after the chided one left. "They consider philosophy to be a gentle intellectual setting-up exercise. Their elevated thoughts are carefully unrelated either to the crudity of outward action or to any scouring inner discipline."

Mere book learning was ever incomplete. "Do not confuse understanding with a larger vocabulary," Yukteswar warned. "Sacred writings are beneficial in stimulating desire for inward realization, if one stanza at a time is slowly assimilated. Otherwise, continual intellectual study may result in vanity, false satisfaction, and undigested knowledge.

"When your conviction of a truth is not merely in your brain but in your being, you may diffidently vouch for its meaning."[18] Book knowledge was not necessary to spiritual realization.

To Your Experience,

Anselam

Driven to Drugs and Books

Dear Arn,

No, Sai Baba was not attracted to learning or scholarship either, because they inclined one towards egoism and pride.

"I must tell you that scholarship in the *Sastras* [spiritual sciences] will not help you," said he; "scholarship is a very dangerous thing for it makes you aware of your ego all the time, instead of helping you to overcome it. If you notice serried ranks of bottles on the shelves of a man, you can conclude that he is a chronic invalid, addicted to drugs. So too, if you see on a man's shelves serried ranks of books, you can conclude that he is a chronic invalid, suffering from doubt and despair and confusion, and addicted to the drugs that he believes will cure them. Like all longstanding invalids, both these will start giving, at the slightest provocation, tedious accounts of their illnesses and the methods by which they tried to cure themselves.

"Want of steady faith is what drives people to drugs and books."[19]

"Practice – that is the real thing in spiritual matters. Scholarship is a burden, it is very often a handicap. So long as God is believed to be far away, in temples and holy places, Man will feel religion a burden and a hurdle. But plant him in your heart and you feel light, burdenless, and even strong. It is like the food basket; when carried on the shoulder, it feels heavy; you are too weak even to carry it. But, sit near a stream and eat it. Though the total weight has not decreased, you feel lighter and stronger. That is the consequence of taking the food *in*: do likewise, with the idea of God. Do not carry it on the shoulder, have it '*in*.'"[20]

You see, scholars so often totter around with weighty conclusions in their minds and stacks of erudition on their shoulders.

Is your status as an academic related to your opposition to the principal, Arn?

Blessings,

Anselam

An Intellectual's Gita

Dear Arn,

My last question surprised you. You don't really see a disadvantage in scholasticism, or erudition, do you?

Let me tell another story, about Pandit Veerabhadra Sarma, the great Vedic scholar and renowned orator, who could expound the sacred scriptures with crystal clarity and vivid eloquence. A minstrel, a poet, a writer, he had achieved every honor in life and every recompense but material wealth.

So acute was his poverty that he blamed Sai Baba for spurning him and loading upon him grief after grief. Seeing his misjudgment, his wife offered to write Baba for relief. But Sarma would have nothing of it. "No prayer should proceed from either of us to Baba, who has mercilessly betrayed our trust," he declared on January 20, 1962. Sensing his ire at that very moment, eight hundred miles away, Baba drafted a letter that reached Sarma on the 23rd. It was an intellectual's Gita, a song of empathic counsel to the piqued scholar.

"Deer child Veerabhadram!" it read. "You are *bhadram* [secure, happy, full of confidence and joy], aren't you? You might ask, 'what kind of *bhadram* is this?' Of course, that question is natural.

"When life flows clear and smooth with no hurdles to cross, to feel that it is so because of oneself and to forget God, and when that flow encounters obstacles and obstructions at every turn, to lament and lose heart – are these not signs of the intellectual frailty inherent in man? You, too, are human, dear *Bhadram*, therefore it is no wonder that you are overcome by depression and despair when troubles bother and obstruct you at every step.

"Though the life of man is basically a manifestation of Immortality and an unbroken stream of *ananda* [bliss], he strays away from the awareness of the *atman* [the inner Spirit] the spring of that *ananda*, slavishly yielding to the vagaries of the mind, the intellect and the ego. Sinking and floating, rising and falling on the turbid waves of the sea of delusion, he is tossed between anxiety and calm, grief and joy, pain and pleasure. He is afflicted with the evanescence of the world and the unreality of his desires.

"Why are you confounded and confused by this false panorama? Remember, you are thereby despising and denying your own atmic identity. You have stored in your brain the Vedas, the Sastras, the Puranas, the Ithihasas, and the Upanishads, but you behave like a dull boor. You bewail your lot and weep at your plight as if you had no resources to fall back upon. This attitude is not worthy of the learning you have accumulated. You have to draw strength and courage therefrom and further the blossoming of holy, heartening thoughts.

"Should this one single trouble – want of money – make you stoop in weakness and fear? You have with you the Name which is the *Dhanavanthri* (Divine Physician) for all the ills and anxieties of man. Instead of letting that Name dance joyously on your tongue, why are you paying so much attention to what you call loss, grief and worry?

"You are the repository of so many branches of scriptural scholarship, but you have neither realized their value nor attempted to experience the joy they can give you. This must be your prime goal. Instead, you are spending your days in the mere satisfaction of having acquired this knowledge, as if fluent oratory were the best purpose to which you could devote your learning.

The result is that you are led into the baseless belief of being attacked by anxieties and adversities.

"Really speaking, these are all objective phenomena, passing clouds that are but a feature of the external nature. The *ananda* that the *atman* can confer on you cannot be lessened or hindered in the least. Have firm faith in this truth. Don't you know, *bangaroo* [meaning gold, applied to a child who is charming and well-behaved], the freedom, the delight and the tranquility you can derive by contemplation of the *ananda* that the unbroken awareness of the *atman* can endow you with? Knowing this, even if you are confronted by the seemingly most insurmountable problem, how can you get entangled with or be affected by circumstances and phenomena in the objective world?

"To preach to others is quite easy, but to put even a fraction of what is preached into actual practice and experience the felicity promised, is extremely difficult. You have been announcing in ringing tones that 'Swami knows everything; Swami is the unitive embodiment of all the names and forms by which man has adored God down the ages.' But when problems overwhelm you, you forget to establish these truths in your own life.

"Don't I know? The other day, when you had been reduced to plead with your father for help and when you were about to proceed to where he resides, your wife suggested, 'we shall write to Swami about our troubles and losses,' let Me ask why you told her, 'I won't allow this; you should not write'? I shall even tell you the reason. You thought she might inform Me about various other details. Don't I know? Can I know this only if she writes to Me? Foolish *bangaroo*! "Don't I know that you went to Ramachandrapuram to give a series of talks on the Gita and returned with a minus balance? The Gita discourses did not receive the response you expected because your talk was pervaded and polluted by the *Burrakatha* style that has long struck root in you [a narration accompanied by song that oft had a socio-political message; it was banned by the British in India]. It cannot be easily overcome. Bear with it patiently and, with steady effort, be rid of it. If you desire that your Gita lectures be appreciated, some improvements are called for. Without effecting them, why do you moan, be gloomy and dejected, blaming your scholarship and your experience as mere useless loads.

"Well, for Me, who is fostering all these worlds, fostering you and your family is no burden. I am giving you these series of troubles in order to teach you some lessons. Study is not all-important. Practising what you have learnt is very necessary. My purpose is to bring to your notice this facet of the process of learning.

"Let me tell you this. He who plants a sapling cannot but water it; if he had no will to water it, he would not have planted it at all . . . Be bold; be in bliss; take up the burden of the duties assigned to you . . . I will never give you up. I will not forget you, no, never.

"You have been maligning the rich; give up this erroneous habit. Not only the rich but you should not dishonour any one in any way. If they are bloated in their ego, *they* will suffer. How can it affect you? Remember, Sai resides in all; so maligning another means maligning Sai Himself.

"Convey my blessings to your wife and children. I have written this long letter out of the compassion and love that I bear towards you. Be ever in joy; be ever intent on practice and experience. The Resident of your heart, Sai."[21]

Love,

Anselam

Yogananda on Negativity

Dear Arn,

Academics are trained in disputation, contention, argumentation, and among the best arguers are historians who mount their claims on the siege towers of history, something non-historians cannot do as well. Your breed are forever inventing new interpretations, and the new interpretations always attack old ones, and the attacks are always justified, say the attackers.

Now you have been attacking your principal by day and night, and you suggest that subversive night time attacks are justified because you also are smiting him to his face. If the attacks are true, you say, it matters not how they are launched.

Master Yogananda, who created the Self-Realization Fellowship in the United States, always disadvised negativity, even in a sound cause. His disciple, J. Donald Walters, recalled that once "a certain man tried by trickery to hurt the work in one of our churches. Mr. Jacot, a loyal and devoted member, uncovered the man's schemes and denounced him publicly. Master expressed his gratitude to Mr. Jacot afterwards for having saved us from a perilous situation. After thanking him, however, he gently scolded him for the means he had employed.

"'It is not good,' he said, 'regardless of one's intentions, to create wrong vibrations through anger and harsh words. The good that you have accomplished would have been greater had you employed peaceful means.'

"Negativity, from whatever motive, creates its own momentum," said Walters. "Unfortunately, Mr. Jacot failed, even after Master's admonishment, to see the need for curbing righteous anger in defense of a good cause. Thus he gradually developed a judgmental mood that ultimately separated him from the work."

"On another occasion," added Walters, "I was invited by a certain Masonic lodge, to which one of our members belonged, to appear in a tableau that was to be presented on the occasion of their installation of officers. Master told me to go. The affair went smoothly enough until the time came for the installation ceremony itself. And then smoldering rivalries burst into flame. Half the lodge members walked out in angry protest. The ceremony ended in emotional ashes.

"'How did it go?' Master inquired of me the following day.

"'Not too well,' I replied.

"'It was a fiasco, wasn't it?'

"'Completely, Sir, I'm afraid!'

"'Well,' he concluded, 'don't say anything about it.'

"His wish that I say nothing at first surprised, and then impressed me. It surprised me because, no matter what I might say, the Masons would never get wind of my remarks. Nor did their internal problems at all affect us. But then I realized that what Master was warning me about was the power of negativity itself.

"'Avoid speaking negative things,' he said to us one evening. 'Why look at the drains, when there is beauty all around? You could take me into the most perfect room in the world, and still, if I wanted to, I would be able to find faults in it. But why should I want to? Why not enjoy its beauty?'[22]

With Affection,

Anselam

P.S. Medicos demonstrate that strongly aggressive and hostile people are seven times more likely to die of heart attacks than the non-aggressive and non-hostile. Married women have stronger immune systems than unmarried ones, and happily married women have stronger systems yet. Those who have lost a spouse are more inclined to illness. Pessimists have more colds than optimists.[23] Negativity in its myriad forms – dullness, despair, defeat, scorn, hate, fraud, glut, rancor, rot, envy, treachery, irreverence, irresolution, loneliness, joylessness, blame, bitterness, disagreeableness, boredom, vulgarity, and a hundred other grim faces – is always life-ebbing, life-denying.

Payoffs of Negativity

Dear Arn,

You ask why negativity even exists, given its pains and penalties.

The answer is that people see payoffs in their negativity. Millions have died for the pleasure of "being right." Countless numbers find pleasure in their own stubbornness or resentment, or contrariness. The thinking takes this turn – "I may be stubborn, but that stubbornness is me, and it has borne fruit, and I enjoy your frustration with my stubbornness. You see, it's a way I control you, and control I relish." Or, "I may have this resentment, but I love expressing it well." Or, "I may be as ornery as an ass, but I'm a *consistent* ass, an ass to everyone, including myself." Or, "I may be hemorrhoidal, but when I wince in the saddle, I sense from you a pleasing waft of sympathy."

Even defeat and loss, paradoxically, can be gratifying as earned punishment or as "proof" of the proclaimed cruelty of fate. This twisted thinking might unravel as: "I told you the world was awful – look what happened to me! I was drawn and quartered! But I'm rather pleased at that, so I could show you graphically my point! It *was* awful, the world *is* awful, and now perhaps you will believe me." Or, "I told you firearms are dangerous. Now I've shot my foot off . . . Do I make myself clear?"

Painfully Yours,

Anselam

Revolt is a weakness – it is the feeling of an impotent will.

the Mother

The Power and Wisdom of a Revolt

Dear Arn,

A crisis looms, a revolt against your principal is possible. You agree with the rebels that the man is incompetent, uninterested, arbitrary. The mathematician does not share your interest in history, and he remains sealed in his office before his computer while disorder reigns in the halls and discouragement seeps into the classrooms. You feel foiled, frustrated. You worry the night through, you wonder what position to take.

May I relate the crisis to the Power and Wisdom? Let's begin with something the Mother said about revolt:

"Basically, disgust, revolt, anger, all these movements of violence are necessarily movements of ignorance and limitation, with all the weakness that limitation represents. Revolt is a weakness – it is the feeling of an impotent will. You will – or you think you will – you feel, you see that things are not as they should be and you revolt against whatever does not agree with what you see. But if you were all-powerful, if your will and your vision were all-powerful, there would be no occasion for you to revolt, you would always see that all things are as they should be. If we go to the highest level and unite with the consciousness of the supreme Will [the Power and Wisdom], we see, at every second, at every moment of the universe, that all is exactly as it should be, exactly as the Supreme wills it. That is omnipotence. And all movements of violence become not only unnecessary but utterly ridiculous.

"Therefore there is only one solution: to unite ourselves by aspiration, concentration, interiorisation and identification with the supreme Will [of the Power and Wisdom]. And that is both omnipotence and perfect freedom at the same time. And that is the only omnipotence and the only freedom; everything else is an approximation. So if you experience this, you realize that with this supreme freedom and supreme power there is also a total peace and a serenity that never fails. Therefore, if you feel something which is not that, a revolt, a disgust, something which you cannot accept, it means that in you there is a part which has not been touched by the transformation, something which has kept the old consciousness, something which is still [off] the path – that is all."[24]

Let me explain.

When you are the Power and Wisdom of your Spirit Self, you are free because you are not assailed by restrictions and limitations. You are not angry with the world, or consumed with changing others. You are right with yourself, and the world is as it needs be. The only way you can be free is by *being the Power*. The Power is the creative force, and if you can create a reality of complete inner assurance, you are free. Only if you *cannot create* your reality are you unfree; only if you remain as Rumi's embryo are you unfree, and unexplored and unrealized.

When you are the Power and Wisdom, how could petty annoyances trouble you? For what reason would you launch a revolt? How could something disgust you? What "wrongness" could anger you?

If you were the Power, things would be right, your world would look right. You would sleep, nothing could disturb you. No countering will could upset you, no quibbling animosity could vex you, no obsession with error could frustrate you. If you were the Power and Wisdom, what could you be angry about? What violence would you feel driven to commit?

Affectionately,

Anselam

P.S. Can you not improve your relationship with this man? You have your preferences, he has his. You do everything weeks in advance, he does everything the last minute. Do what you need to do, understanding he will do the same. If you need his OK on a letter for students and parents, prepare the letter in your way, in advance, and given his past approval, you will likely have little trouble, and if he wants something worthy added, add it. If you get angry that he is not like you, what freedom have you given *him*?

If you begin to see that things are well and as they should be, when formerly they seemed askew and disturbed, that is a welcome sign . . .

Passivity invites aggression.

David R. Hawkins

Peace, Not Pacifism

Dear Arn,

Take not from the Mother a counsel of pacifism – your highest Voice may advise confrontation.

Two thoughts about action with your principal . . .

Sai Baba:
"Education . . . should confer on the student the courage to stand up against injustice, indiscipline, immorality and falsehood."[25]

David R. Hawkins:
"A yardstick that is helpful in making decisions is to project oneself ahead to one's deathbed and ask which decision do I want to be accountable for at that time."[26]

The Masters always encouraged peace, but not passivity or pacifism. In *The Bhagavad Gita* before the great Kurukshetra War between the Pandava brothers and their evil cousins, the Kauravas, Arjuna, the Pandava archer, did not want to fight against his own family, friends, and teacher. But he had to take a stand, while still loving them.

"From the moment of conception to the surrender of the last breath, man has to fight in each incarnation innumerable battles – biological, hereditary, bacteriological, physiological, climatic, social, ethical, political, sociological, psychological, metaphysical so many varieties of inner and outer conflicts," said Yogananda. "Competing for victory in every encounter are the forces of good and evil. The whole intent of the Gita is to align man's efforts on the side of *dharma*, or righteousness. The ultimate aim is Self-realization, the realization of man's true Self, the soul, as made in the image of God, one with the ever-existing, ever-conscious, ever-new bliss of Spirit."[27]

Many spiritual people are confounded by war. "The most common error," Master Hawkins said, "is to misidentify spirituality as passivity and thus aid, abet, and invite aggression. From history, as well as consciousness calibration, we see that passivity encourages aggression and thus represents weakness and not moral superiority."[28]

At lower levels of consciousness, embracing eighty-five percent of the world's population, "the strong attack the weak," said Hawkins; at higher levels, "the strong protect the weak."[29] Tyrants, like Hitler and Himmler and Stalin and Beria, and numerous others, subsisted at the base levels of brutality. Faced with pacifism, they routinely answered with savagery. The high hopes of "principled" pacifists that if we be nice to them, they will be nice to us, were fantasy. "Grandiose, 'macho' dictators," said Hawkins, "despise such weak 'feminine,' 'cowardly' positions and are, in fact, further inflamed into aggression" by their own primitive, predatory instincts . . . i.e. "Passivity invites aggression."[30]

Thus Hitler and his cronies laughed when Chamberlain offered appeasement at Munich instead of resistance.

Issues with your principal are not as serious, but they do require resolution, so ask the Power and Wisdom, as Arjuna asked Krishna, for that resolution. The asking is the first action; following the advice is the second.

To Peace,

Anselam

The Smothering Robe of Virtue

Dear Arn,

How will you hear the Voice, you ask.

There are steps to enlightenment . . .

It is not normally possible to move directly to the heeding of the Voice of God in all matters. What seems to happen first is the creation of a moral code where one takes a stand for certain principles and holds strongly against any perversion of them or outright disregard for them. Then a major step is taken to surrender all moral (and other issues) to the Power and Wisdom or to God. But only a tiny, tiny minority reach this last stage. Why? Because a goodly number have not even got to the principled stage. The Buddha once said, "rare it is and extremely fortunate to be born a human . . . Rarer still is it to hear of the Truth, and even rarer yet is it to pursue the Truth . . ."[31]

Now those who want to hear the truth and to pursue it usually do so a bit at a time . . . They may become aware of a higher Self, a Power and Wisdom, a Spirit or God, but almost always the ego powerfully resists the relinquishing one's whole life to the divine impulse. Even Aurobindo said that had he been asked to do it all at once, he'd have failed.[32] The resistance of the ego can take the form of a forceful declaration that whatever principle it holds is right and must be defended to the death. The ego can be very self-righteous, standing like the God it wants to be even against the God that Is. It will even assert that its principles are God-given; its morality, God's own . . .

Ironically, then, an absolute insistence on some moral

code, and the world has had scores of codes, can prevent further growth; if the insistence is not released, it will prevent enlightenment. It is the error of taking any stage as the final step, something Aurobindo warned strongly against.[33]

There is a resistance to going further, a resistance to handing oneself over to the Divine, as if one will be blown away by this giant tsunami and lose all that he deems his "personality." This opposition to Truth causes discomfort – clinging to what was and impeding what might be – the two great sources of pain.

Then the few that say they are handing their lives over to the Divine, often hand parts over with conditions. And in effect, they approach God with these conditions.

A soldier might say, "Advise me, Father, but honor my devotion to duty . . . My first precept, and I am sworn to it, is loyalty to the state. Tell me whatever, Lord, but if you say, 'break that oath,' I won't do it. It's who I am; it's my identity. You can suggest, you can pester, you can importune, but if you say 'be someone else, something different,' I won't listen."*

Or, a person in marital difficulty might say, "Advise me, God, but honor my fixed obligations. If you say break off the relationship, and I declare it my painful duty to continue, I won't hear you."

Or, "If Lord, you tell me to do something that counters my notion of virtue, I decline. Please approach me with *my* notion, not yours."

Or, "If you tell me to go to war against some monstrous evil, and I be an ardent pacifist, a 'principled' pacifist, I double-decline. Please understand *my* notion of peace, not yours, or perhaps better, yours in *light* of mine."

These conditions require God to agree with your ego,

your intellect, your judgments, for anything less insults the ego, attacks the "personality" you have so painstakingly rigged.

Now if you say: "Lord, tell me anything you want, but don't ask me to run against my priorities, my preferences, my preconceptions, my prejudices" – you would hardly have surrendered.

Thus the last ones to surrender are often the unbendingly "virtuous."

Note also that the notion of surrender is frightening to any earthly authority, like an army, a church, a judiciary, even a school system, because the higher Self, and the Divine of which it is a part, are not subject to those authorities, however well-intentioned they be.

One day Aurobindo explained this in a simple epigram:

"My lover took away my robe of sin, and I let it fall, rejoicing; then he plucked at my robe of virtue, but I was ashamed and alarmed and prevented him. It was not till he wrested it from me by force that I saw how my soul had been hidden from me."[34]

You are very principled, Arn. Has your robe of virtue muffled your inner voice? Doffing the robe, can you hear better?

With Affection,

Anselam

* This very principle of loyalty to the state and its head prevented many German officers from removing Hitler, even after they recognized his insanity and barbarity. Could the Power and Wisdom actually advise the execution of such a madman? Perhaps . . .

Aurobindo once declared shockingly, "He who will not slay when God bids him, works in the world an incalculable havoc."[35] Ever interpreting Aurobindo, the Mother was asked, "In what . . . circumstances does God give the command to slay?" and she replied, "This is a question I cannot answer, because God has never asked me to slay."[36] But Arn, study Claus von Stauffenberg, who attempted to kill Hitler on July 20, 1944, and you may have an example of where God asked just that. "Fate has offered us the opportunity, and I would not refuse it for anything in the world," Stauffenberg stated. "I have examined myself before God and my conscience. It must be done as this man is evil personified."[37]

Stauffenberg failed, but perchance the Lord had something grander in mind.

"The world has had only half a dozen successful revolutions and most even of these were very like failures," wrote Aurobindo; "yet it is by great and noble failures that humanity advances."[38] The Mother explained: "It is not success that confers greatness but the motive of the action and the nobleness of the feelings which inspire it."[39]

You may be surprised that not many take a stand for themselves, Arn, for their own higher consciousness, for the Spirit they want to be, the reality they want to create. You cannot reach enlightenment until you take that stand. It means being loyal to your Spirit Self, to your richest impulses. It requires iron determination and indomitable courage. I have little thought about whether Stauffenberg reached enlightenment when he did what he did, but I do know that in taking a stand for himself, he took a very necessary step . . .

But I digress . . .

Virtue an Obstacle?

Dear Alma,

May I go into the matter of virtue?

You say other teachers do not emphasize virtue the way you do. You say it shows in their students' and their children's behavior, in the "simple and mindless" lack of consideration for others. Some of your "friends" don't return phone calls or e-mails the way you do; most don't clean up their homerooms or the staffroom the way you do. Two or three you cannot count on. Lacking "true responsibility" they perpetuate this thoughtlessness among their students in returning assignments and assessments weeks late, in one case two months late. And you end your outpouring wondering if you have become too self-righteous!

Well, you are onto something, because if so, your "virtue" is in danger.

"Self-righteousness is the worst enemy of virtue," Aurobindo said. And the Mother explained that self-righteousness was "a feeling of virtuous superiority. Your virtue makes you disdainful of others, and this pride – which fills you with disdain for those who, according to you, are less virtuous than you are – makes your virtue completely worthless."[40]

You have a great need to be virtuous, Alma. You have said so more than once, and you think our "literary exchanges" have eased you that way. But what your notion of virtue would *have* you do, and what the Divine would *suggest* you do are often quite different. For across cultures and time, human virtues have been strikingly variable, and strikingly intolerant. “Virtue has always spent its time eliminating whatever it found bad in life,” said the Mother, “and if all the virtues of the various countries of the world had been put together, very few things would remain in existence.”[41]

In a rant, Robert Ingersoll declared: “Men and women have been burned for thinking there is but one God; that there was none; that the Holy Ghost is younger than God; that God was somewhat older than his son; for insisting that good works will save a man without faith; that faith will do without good works; for declaring that a sweet babe will not be burned eternally because its parents failed to have its head wet by a priest; for speaking of God as though he had a nose; for denying that Christ was his own father; . . . for pretending that priests can forgive sins; . . . for doubting the total depravity of the human heart; . . . for thinking the Virgin Mary was born like other people; for thinking that a man’s rib was hardly sufficient to make a good-sized woman; . . . for asserting that prayers are not answered, that diseases are not sent to punish unbelief; for denying the authority of the Bible; for having a Bible in their possession; for attending mass, and for refusing to attend; for carrying a cross and for refusing; for being a Catholic, and for being a Protestant; for being an Episcopalian, a Presbyterian, a Baptist, and for being a Quaker. In short, every virtue has been a crime, and every crime a virtue.”[42]

Now I do not mean there is no truth or no right way. The good is the right way. “The good is what works is a sound though insufficient statement,” says Jesus of *A Course in Miracles*. “Only the good *can* work; nothing else works at all.”[43] But ultimately, the good requires not the constriction of a human precept, but the immensity of the Divine Power and Wisdom.

Now carry this notion of the good, or of virtue, *as the human sees it*, further. In one of her arresting assertions, the Mother said, "The need to be virtuous is *the greatest obstacle* to self-giving."[44] Strange as it sounds, she meant that when you surrender to the Power and Wisdom, to the Divine, you must not carry with you your notions of good and bad, what you will accept and what you won't. You are surrendering to the Power, not dictating to it. A priest, for example, may swear an oath of chastity, and in surrendering he might really be saying: "I surrender myself to Thee, Lord, but You must take me, virtues intact. I have already determined what I will not do. As a priest, I have taken a vow of chastity, and I cannot possibly conceive in the infinity of Your wisdom a circumstance in which my infinite love might be expressed through sex." Well, if there is an infinity of wisdom directing, and an infinity of love expressing, it is conceivable, though not certain, that the Divine might so direct his affection. But he has already ruled it out because it is not part of his conception of virtue. The need to be virtuous has thus become an obstacle to his self-giving.

But let us not pick on priests. Anyone who is convinced of his own virtue could well be surprised when he meets his Maker. Imagine the perplexity and shock of a Puritan who surrendered himself to a God of *Delight* – he would likely take offence to all that delight, all that joy, and could even wonder how he might covert God to his more somber and depressing view of what God should be. You can see that his idea of virtue would be more than "the greatest obstacle to self-giving," or self-surrender; it would completely negate it.

Or imagine Torquemada, father of the Spanish Inquisition, surrendering himself to the Divine, only to discover that God was a God of love! Or consider a thrall, working Torquemada's thumbscrews in some dungeon, discovering that cruelty was a "vibration" infinitely distant from the Lord's. There would no doubt be disappointment at God's failure to meet the proper standards.

Genuine virtue is only possible through the superconscious mind, the mind of Spirit.

To Clarity,

Anselam

P.S. H.L. Mencken defined Puritanism as "the haunting fear that someone, somewhere, may be happy."[45]

Rules, Rules, Rules

Dear Alma,

How rigorously should you hold to a rule, a man-made, or woman-made rule?

In the deep ferment of the late 1960s, when every rule and regulation, every social convention, every establishment tradition and creed was being turfed, someone asked the Mother – "Is it good to break all moral and social conventions as the new generation is doing? Don't these things have any value?"

The Mother answered – "What has value at one period no longer has any at another, as human consciousness goes on progressing. But one must take great care to replace a law one no longer obeys by a higher and truer law that fosters progress towards the future realization. One has no right to abandon a law until one is capable of knowing and following a higher and better law."[46]

Notice that most people are fledgling law-makers, counseled by their prejudices and braced by their whims. Judgement upon judgement they pass in the courts of gossip, sternly, self-righteously, rigidly, pitilessly, upon everyone and everything, upon what the others are, what others have done and what they might do. At one point, when the rock and roll band, The Rolling Stones, were still playing forty-five years after their inception, one of these judgements fell from this lower court of caprice, the mass notion of rightness – the band was too old, they must retire. But for all his warts, Mick Jagger was following a higher law.

"I know there's a lot of talk about that [retirement]," said he. "But those are rules bureaucrats make. If you're an artist, poet or musician, other things matter. We have the feeling we're still a very good band, and we love what we're doing. Besides that, I'm a terrible plumber. There's nothing else I could do."[47]

Father De Mello followed his heart too.

"For all his traditional ways," De Mello wrote, "the Master had scant respect for rules and for traditions." When a disciple demanded that his daughter bow to his wishes regarding a mate, as required by religious rule, the Master sided openly with the daughter. And when the disciple asked what kind of holy man would trample a tradition, the Master replied, "You must understand that life is just like music, which is made more by feeling and by instinct than by rules."[48]

Love,

Anselam

P.S. Arn might like this story of Mirabeau, the French revolutionary: students were viewing the French Assembly in disgust at the interminable debate and argument. "Laws are like sausages," Mirabeau told them. "You should never watch them being made."[49]

Obsessiveness

Dear Alma,

Good, you have seen a habit others have noted in you before – you tend to overdo things. You check to see if your doors are locked, three or four times; you check to see if you have the tickets to a show, three or four times. You ask someone to do something, but you ask several times, and fearing default, you ask again. Hardly self-trust, you say! "Pest," your colleagues whisper.

Copying you, Larah feels the worry, and copying my own mother, I felt it every time we went out and she looked at the controls on the stove and said, "off, off, off, off, off," then repeated herself going in reverse.

Obsessiveness is common – not one car but three, not one tuxedo but four, not one pair of shoes but ten, not one lover, but many.

Harpo Marx, the Marx brother who feigned dumbness, was once afflicted by a woman utterly insistent that he appear at a New York charity. In forty-eight hours, she called him twelve times. Obsessed that he might squirm away, she called to escort him to the benefit. As they left the hotel room, the phone rang. "Don't you want to go back and answer it?" the obsessive asked. "Why bother?" groaned Harpo. "It's undoubtedly you again."[50]

And, very good, you have noticed that Obsessions don't listen. They can't hear beyond their own voice, they can't see beyond their own form – they are blocked, stifled. An obsession only wants to see and hear itself, so it is a refusal to expand, an example of how clinging prevents growth. It makes a person one-dimensional, absolutely predictable, and quite boring.

Not many have this insight. Good for you!

To Equal-mindedness,

Anselam

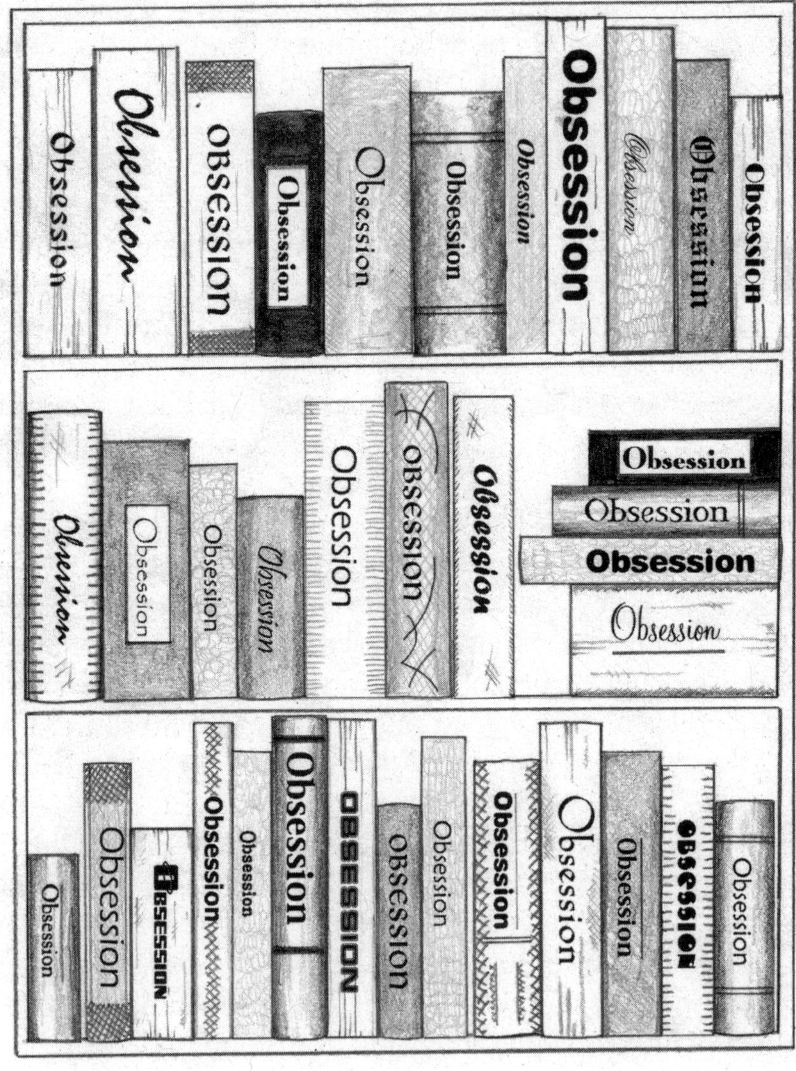

Infatuation

Dear Alma,

I pray this may help with young Larah who has fallen in love, for infatuation is a cousin of obsession.

David R. Hawkins, a Master of the Academy, using kinesiological testing, calibrated the level of consciousness of everything from shame to courage to love and unconditional love on a logarithmic scale from 0 to 1000. The levels of falsehood that people live as their dominant experience include shame, guilt, hatred, grief, and anger, ranging from 20 to 175. The levels of truth that others live begins with courage at 200, ranging upward through reason, love, joy, peace and enlightenment at 700. Masters like Jesus, Krishna, Buddha and Zoroaster stood at the highest level on this plane: 1000.

Eighty-five percent of the world's population operates below the crucial level of 200; only 4 percent reach the stage of Love at 500; and only .4 of one percent reach Unconditional love, at 540.[51]

There is a considerable difference between Love at 500 and infatuation that calibrates at only 145. Master Hawkins explained:

· The locus of infatuation is partially in the ego;
the locus of love is in the big Self, in Spirit.

· The intention of infatuation derives from the
mating instinct, to get a mate; the intention of love
is to bond and enjoy.

· The duration of infatuation is transitory; the duration of love is permanent.

· The passion of infatuation releases adrenaline and sex hormones; the experience of love releases endorphins that create joy.

· The emotion of infatuation can be frantic, fearful, frustrating, even tormenting, especially if loss is contemplated. Infatuation often summons anxiety. The emotion of love is self-fulfilling and satisfying, and it summons gratitude.

· Body functions during infatuation are often impaired, with loss of appetite and loss of sleep. Body functions at the level of love are improved.

· With infatuation, judgment is impeded; with love it is enhanced.

· With infatuation, the intention is often to possess, to capture, to control, to own; with love is to "be with."

· With infatuation one's productivity is disrupted; with love, it is enriched.

· With infatuation, the sense of balance is erratic; with love it is steady.

· With infatuation, the sense of loss is often accompanied by rage, hate, blame. With love, loss is experienced as grief, regret, or longing.

· Infatuation that is unrequited and unreturned, has a pathology that includes despair, depression, stalking, even suicide. Love has none of those attributes.[52]

Some people feel that this infatuation phase is indispensable to real love, that without it marriage cannot exist, affection is superficial, happiness is impossible, and togetherness, unthinkable. Some, even those in beautiful relationships now, feel cheated that they never experienced with their spouses this fleeting moment of frenzy and fancy. Others long for it again with all its derangement and disorientation, overvaluing a vanishing pebble as if it were a pearl. Preceding breakup as oft as bliss, infatuation never was love, and, without vast unfolding, never could be.

I shall convey the heart of this to Larah who has asked about love. It may help her, but remember, this is her first experience.

To Love,

Anselam

The Agony or the Joy of Competition

Dear Arn,

You have always been competitive, and competition has exhausted you. You want to win so badly you can't enjoy any game. Most sports you play reasonably well – until you have to make a shot. Then fear grips you, tension wracks you, and you can't control the *subtlety* required, from a putt in golf to a finger flick in crokinole. When you miss an easy one under pressure, you beat yourself up. And you go to the trouble of remembering all those times you missed, and all those beatings, and all that dejection, and all that self-doubt and self-anger. Not surprisingly, you want to experience competition differently, but you don't know how.

Bill Russell, the great basketball player for the Boston Celtics from 1956-1969, won eleven NBA championships. He was an NBA all-star twelve times, MVP five times. A magnificent defensive artist, he is one of only two players to have gathered fifty rebounds in a single game. Unknown and sadly unvalued by most sports fans, was the fact that Russell had transcended the negative aspects of competition. To me, that was his greatest achievement.

"The game would be in a white heat of competition, and yet somehow I wouldn't feel competitive – which is a miracle in itself," he wrote. " I'd be putting out the maximum effort, straining, coughing up parts of my lungs as we ran, and yet I never felt the pain. The game would move so quickly that every fake, cut, and pass would be surprising, and yet nothing could surprise me. It was almost as if we were playing in slow motion. During those spells I could almost sense how the next play would develop and where the next shot would be taken. Even before the other team brought the ball in-bounds, I could feel it so keenly that I'd want to shout to my teammates, 'It's coming there!' – except that I knew everything would change if I did. My premonitions would be consistently correct, and I always felt then that I not only knew all the Celtics by heart but also all the opposing players, and that they all knew me. There have been many times in my career when I felt moved or joyful, but these were the moments when I had chills pulsing up and down my spine . . . On the five or ten occasions when the game ended at that special level, I literally did not care who had won. If we lost, I'd still be as free and high as a sky hawk."[53]

Perhaps this example of a man you idolize in sports history will help, Arn, and there is something in this story for Sanson too.

Love,

Anselam

The Ways of Resolution

Dear Arn,

Interesting how your revolt against the principal turned out . . . You prayed for help. The poor man developed carpal tunnel syndrome from uninterrupted computer typing, required an operation, then unexpectedly resigned, aggrieved that his core delight in administration was scotched!

You remind me of Father Divine, the African-American revivalist, whose congregation was so uproarious he was sued by neighbors. On November 16, 1931, Justice Lewis J. Smith fined the pastor $500 and slapped him with a six-month jail term. Four days later, Justice Smith shockingly dropped dead, and reporters rushed for Divine's reaction. The amiable preacher shook his head, "I just hated to do it."[54]

Actually, you approached the revolt correctly and asked the Power and Wisdom within to resolve the matter for *you*. That is, you wanted a resolution that would please you, satisfy you, not one that demanded that *he* apologize, change, or make amends. The Power and Wisdom is a power over your own myopia, your own misgiving, not over anyone else's. It corrects your vision, makes your peace. But it can do so in strange ways, as testified by your kind visits to the man in recovery.

That is how to pray when you want change. It is also what to request when you worry about Larah's future career. Ask that her choices will be right with you, ask that *your* worry be resolved, that *your* attitude be enlightened.

To Resolution,

Anselam

Owning Your Faults

Dear Alma and Arn,

The resolution of your worry and the enlightenment of your attitude usually reveal faults and foibles.

But character defects tend to diminish as soon as they are acknowledged and owned.

Master Hawkins once told us:

"The benefit of accepting one's defects instead of denying them is an increase in an inner sense of self-honesty, security and higher self-esteem, accompanied by greatly diminished defensiveness. A self-honest person is not prone to having their feelings hurt by others, and therefore, honest insight has an immediate benefit in the reduction of actual as well as potential emotional pain. A person is vulnerable to emotional pain in exact relationship to the degree of self-awareness and self-acceptance. When we admit our downside, others cannot attack us there. As a consequence, we feel emotionally less vulnerable, and more safe and secure. Most domestic arguments stem from the refusal to own or take responsibility for even simple character defects, such as forgetting an errand or some triviality, which, oddly enough, constitutes the majority of interpersonal conflict. Most bickering represents the endless accusations over trivialities that emotional maturity and honesty would have prevented in the first place. Battered spouses and marital homicide start out over mundane affairs and then escalate as they trigger the release of the narcissistic ego to which 'being right' is astonishingly more important than even life itself."[55]

Tomorrow I will answer your question about Hawkins' background.

Love,

Anselam

Master Hawkins

Dear Alma and Arn,

Hawkins is something like Aurobindo, a student of the world's teachings and a spiritual Master to boot. A medical doctor, a therapist, a scientist, he began psychiatry in 1952. An international authority on human consciousness, he has been knighted and honored in the East as a foremost teacher of enlightenment. His opus, *Power Vs. Force: The Hidden Determinants of Human Behavior* (1995) was followed by a series of penetrating insights in *Truth vs. Falsehood* (2005), *Transcending the Levels of Consciousness – The Stairway to Enlightenment* (2006) and *Discovery of the Presence of God* (2007).[56]

For long, Hawkins operated a vast therapy in the United States with fifty doctors and other helpers, 1000 new patients every year and 2000 outpatients. His service to the mass of sufferers he described:

"Patients came to see me from every country in the world, and some were the most hopeless of the hopeless. Grotesque, writhing, and wrapped in wet sheets for transport from faraway hospitals, they came to me, hoping for treatment for advanced psychoses and grave, incurable mental disorders. Some were catatonic; many had been mute for years. But in each patient, beneath the crippled appearance, I clearly saw the shining essence of love and beauty, perhaps so obscured to ordinary vision that he or she had become totally unloved in this world.

"One day a mute catatonic was brought into the hospital in a straitjacket. She had a severe neurological disorder and was unable to stand – she squirmed on the floor in spasms, and her eyes were rolling back in her head. Her hair was matted and she'd torn all of her clothes and could only utter guttural sounds. Her family was fairly wealthy; therefore, she'd been seen by innumerable physicians over the years, including famous specialists from all over the world. Every treatment had been tried on her, until the medical profession had finally given up, calling her situation 'hopeless.'

"I looked at her and asked nonverbally, 'What do you want me to do with her, God?' I then realized that I was just to love her; that was all. Her inner self shone through her eyes, and I connected with that loving essence. In that second, she was healed by her own recognition of who she really was; what happened to her mind or body didn't matter to her any longer.

"This, in essence, happened with countless patients. Some recovered in the eyes of the world, and some did not, but whether or not a clinical recovery had occurred no longer mattered to the patients. Their inner agony was over; as they felt loved and at peace within, their pain stopped."[57]

To Love,

Anselam

P.S. Hawkins is a knight of the Sovereign Order of the Hospitaliers of St. John of Jerusalem, founded in 1077. Prince Waldemar of Denmark presided at Hawkins's installation in 1995 at the San Anselmo Theological Seminary.

A Noxious Air

Dear Arn,

So your deeply cynical colleague poisons the air, and you can actually smell the rankness, the foulness, the festering, the dis-ease. Very interesting . . . Virtually all can *feel* cynicism, feel the uglification, the deformity, but you are right – there is a dank spoilage about it, a waste and a rot. I knew that you were increasingly clairvoyant and clairaudient, Arn, but now, "clairnasal" as well! What you say is true – every disease has an odor to those sensitive enough to detect it, and indeed a whole new order of healing could be founded upon the *smell* of sickness, a kind of pathology of vapors.

There is much on cynicism in our previous letters in *Meditations*.[58] Recall that cynicism is the belief in the futility of human thought and endeavor. As a plan of action, cynicism is meaningless, because to a cynic nothing bloody works; as a reflection on others it is disparaging, because to a cynic all are fools; and as a judgment on himself, it is equally degrading, because anyone who believes in the futility of his own thought and endeavor must also in the end believe in his own *impotence*.

Well, you might apply love to cynicism, love the cynic, accept him as he is, show him the beauty of your love, the beauty of human affection everywhere, gently help him remove the fear which clogs his arteries, show him you are not afraid, and that he need not be. Do not try to convert him, just love him. Conversion is not love; it forces itself on another. Just radiate affection, beam forth good will.

Help him to love himself more, because if he thinks he is impotent and that the world is fearsome, he does not know himself. A person who thinks he is weak and inconsequential does not love that fabricated aspect of himself; he does not really love what he's made of himself. If he were to love himself as he truly is, he would never be cynical. He would be so filled with good will for himself, so patient, so uncondemning, so calm, so positive, so assured, that he could never again see things as amiss, or himself as handicapped and victimized.

With Affection,

Anselam

Talking Too Much

Dear Larah,

So the love affair was neither an affair nor love. The young man talked too much! Stories about everyone! And not always true.

It reminds me of a word I still love, *logorrhea* – verbal diarrhea.

Mark Twain, whom you enjoy, once talked of this very disease in adults:

"Some years ago in Hartford, we all went to church one hot sweltering night to hear the annual report of Mr. Hawley, a city missionary who went around finding people who needed help and didn't want to ask for it. He told of the life in cellars, where poverty resided; he gave instances of the heroism and devotion of the poor. 'When a man will millions give,' he said, 'we make a great deal of noise. It's noise in the wrong place, for it's the widow's mite that counts.' Well, Hawley worked me up to a great pitch. I could hardly wait for him to get through. I had $400 in my pocket. I wanted to give that and borrow more to give. You could see greenbacks in every eye. But instead of passing the plate then, he kept on talking and talking, and as he talked it grew hotter and hotter, and we grew sleepier and sleepier. My enthusiasm went down, down, down, down – $100 at a clip – until finally, when the plate did come around, I stole ten cents out of it. It all goes to show how a little thing like this can lead to crime."[59]

I'm glad you got something from my little note on infatuation.

To Silence,

Anselam

logorrhea (n.)

... a little thing like this can lead to crime.

Mark Twain

Relief

Dear Arn,

Yes, I have noticed that too – a kind of gravity, seriousness, in your demeanor the last six weeks.

You have taught language arts for seven or eight years now, and I know you appreciate botched metaphors. A former student of mine sent these, apparently from student essays:

> *She grew on him like she was a colony of E. coli and he was room-temperature Canadian beef.*
>
> *She had a deep, throaty, genuine laugh, like that sound a dog makes just before it throws up.*
>
> *He was as tall as a six-foot-three-inch tree.*
>
> *Her hair glistened in the rain, like nose hair after a sneeze.*
>
> *He fell for her like his heart was a mob informant, and she was the East River.*
>
> *The young fighter had a hungry look, the kind you get from not eating for a while.*
>
> *The ballerina rose gracefully en point and extended one slender leg behind her, like a dog at a fire hydrant.*

She walked into my office like a centipede with ninety-eight missing legs.

Her voice had that tense, grating quality, like a generation thermal paper fax machine that needed a band tightened.

It hurt the way your tongue hurts after you accidentally staple it to the wall.[60]

In Fun,

Anselam

Absent-mindedness

Dear Alma,

You spoke of a bout of absent-mindedness.

The former dictator of Greece, General Georges Metaxas, was inspecting a Mediterranean air base by seaplane when he told the co-pilot that he was about to land at the airport.

"Excuse me, General," said the co-pilot courteously, "but it would be better to come down on the sea; this is a seaplane."

"Of course, commander, what was I thinking of," said Metaxas, who then landed beautifully on the Mediterranean.

Rising from the cockpit, Metaxas added, "Commander, I greatly appreciate the tact with which you drew my attention to the incredible blunder that I nearly made."

Then he opened the door and stepped into the sea.[61]

Absent-mindedness indicates that one is not living in the Power, because the Power is active and attentive and lives moment by moment, neither in the past nor the future, but in the present.

To Attention,

Anselam

What Then is Falsehood?

Dear Alma,

Yes, earlier we urged desisting, and you ask what all the desisting amounts to.

Letting go of falsehood.

The Mother once said, "Real Falsehood, the negation of Truth (the WILLED negation of Truth), is to me, something completely black and inert. That's the feeling it gives me. It is black, blacker than the blackest coal, and inert – inert without any response.

"Falsehood proper is this. It is the assertion that the Divine does not exist, Life does not exist, Light does not exist, Love does not exist, Progress does not exist – Light, Life, Love, do not exist."[62]

All these things amount to false beliefs.

The issue of choice and of choosing wisely invariably involves a therapy of beliefs because there are many unwise beliefs and limiting concepts that have to be identified and rejected. Much of what Larry Wayne and Grace Johnston teach is this very therapy.

In their book *Songs from Spirit,* Dr. Bernadt, a physician in spirit, speaks of four levels of conviction: an intellectual understanding, a belief, a faith and a knowing within. These levels are rather like the incoming tide, with intellectual understanding occurring just as the sea turns shoreward and inner knowing occurring when the tide is full. The levels are really fuller and fuller certainties of belief. "The knowing within," said Bernadt, "is the God Power within you, the spirit."

Now, you are not safe until you reach the knowing within, because genuine inner knowing is knowing what is TRUE.

Remember that faith, a very potent form of belief, can be invested in what is false, so faith, without inner knowing is always dangerous. One can have faith in a megalomaniac, a lunatic, or a liar, and history is filled with examples. One can have faith in a placebo too, which is a way of fooling an individual into activating the natural healing power of his being. But genuine inner knowing requires a knowing of what is true. Master N. Sri Ram, a theosophist, once said, "Truth is Life in its highest, most evolved state. Truth, beauty and goodness stand and fall together. One test of Truth, therefore, is goodness; another is beauty. Truth is infinite, and as we delve more deeply into it, we shall find yet greater depths, wider latitudes, and ever-new dimensions. What you are deep within yourself is the Truth of your being. What you seem and do must flow from that Truth and be patterned upon it."[63]

Love,

Anselam

Dangerous Beliefs

Dear Alma and Arn,

All right, more about beliefs . . .

Beliefs are really embryos, unaware that they are embryos. But even an embryo creates its own reality, because it is the part of Love to honor beliefs, for love would not disturb one's faith, if that is where faith has been placed.

Where is the Power the Masters extol? From a purely human perspective, it lies in belief; from the inner Self perspective, it lies in Spirit.

For the power of belief, without a grounding in truth, can be dangerous, even fatal. If you believe you have caused all the unhappiness in your life, but that you cannot cause it to vanish, you will be part potent and part impotent, strong in a negative sense only. If you believe that sorrow is ennobling, and you want to be ennobled, you will summon the catalyst of suffering. If you believe you are at the mercy of outside events, prepare for windstorms and riptides. If you believe that a specific circumstance makes you sad or solemn, it will. If you believe that you must accept your troubles, you may well have them forever. Be careful what you believe, especially if it belittles the majesty of your own Spirit.

A hundred years ago, Walter Cannon of Harvard Medical School revealed the power of taboo amongst the Maoris of New Zealand. In one case, a young, traveling native was at an older friend's home for breakfast when the friend served him wild hen, a dish strictly forbidden to the younger generation. Repeatedly, the young one asked if he were eating hen and was told no. Some years later, the older asked if the younger would now eat wild hen, and the latter said that if it were forbidden he would never touch it. Then the elder one laughed and told him that he had fooled him those many moons ago and had indeed fed him the prohibited hen. The news so distressed the younger man that in twenty-four hours he was dead.[64]

Psychologist Bruno Klopfer once treated a man named Wright in the last stages of cancer. Wright had baseball-sized tumors in his lymph nodes, his spleen and liver were massively enlarged, and his lungs had to be drained of two quarts of fluid daily. Nonetheless, Wright still held hope, and he told his doctor of a miracle drug he had read of – Krebiozen – and he begged for it. The drug was for those with life expectancy of three months, not three days, but the doctor complied one Friday, fully expecting Wright to die over the weekend.

On Monday, however, Wright was up and about, the tumors having "melted like snowballs on a hot stove" to half their original bulk. In ten days, Wright left the hospital, cancer-free. No longer needing oxygen, he flew his own plane, breathing easily at 12 000 feet, and for two months he moved in peace, completely healed.

Then he read claims that Krebiozen was useless in combating lymphatic cancer. Immediately, he fell into depression, and the old sickness returned. This time his doctor told a white lie – it was true, he said, that the Krebiozen was ineffective, but only because it had deteriorated during transit. Now he had the real thing, enhanced and concentrated, and he was ready to inject it on command. Grasping at this new hope, Wright took the needle that unbeknownst to him conveyed only water into his body.

Again the tumors receded, and the cancer vanished. And again Wright was well – for two months – until the American Medical Association announced the complete uselessness of Krebiozen. Utterly broken, Wright filled with cancer and died in two days.[65]

Let me tell another story of the power of belief and the importance of linking belief with Truth, so that Truth may become a knowing within.

Elizabeth Fehr was born in Essen, Germany, in 1920. Fleeing Hitlerism, she emigrated to the United States where she studied psychiatry. One day, a twenty-four-year-old man entered her office, having escaped from a mental hospital after three suicide attempts. Doctors told him that only a lobotomy would short-circuit his incurable psychosis and prevent a lifetime of institutional confinement. The man said he was stuck, as if in a manhole, and he began to writhe and contort, apparently trying to escape. The eel-like twisting reminded Fehr of birthing, and she thought the man was trying to be born, but born right this time. As he slipped to the floor, she went with him and "delivered" him. And there he lay, unstuck at last, at ease, his frenzy abated and psychosis allayed, his desperation over. Later she rebirthed him some more. And he began working, found a girlfriend, and looked completely normal.

Thus began Fehr's natal therapy, which eventually attracted psychiatrist and author R. D. Laing. One night Laing himself "went through," as did a sixteen-year-old female psychotic. "She looked listless, eyes lusterless, skin flat, dry. She writhed, squirmed, contracted, agonized on the floor for about fifteen minutes until she felt she 'came out.'" Laing was astounded at the change in her. "Her eyes were bright, almost glistening. Her skin warm and moist.

She said she realized, with wonder, a feeling she could not remember ever having before." She felt touched. And before, she was torn between a fear of contact and a deep need "to cling." In those minutes, these were gone. And two years later, said Laing, "she was still 'all right.'"

Fehr wrought similar remarkable results in London that Laing witnessed, and he began to incorporate rebirthing into his own clinic.

Underlying the therapy was Fehr's belief that being born was terrifying, that the uterine contractions were like being minced, pulverized, beaten, crushed. The process of birth was stifling, smothering, and from such a horrific beginning human traumas naturally sprang. Even homosexuals could be "cured" of their orientation, if only they realized that the terror of being born had caused their "aberration." Redo the birth, knowing what it had created, and with the knowing a "new" heterosexuality would emerge.

Three months before her death, Elizabeth Fehr was invited to Jane Roberts's home where Roberts was channeling the famous Seth books. Seth and Roberts seem to have been one of those spiritual partnerships, like Jac Purcell and Lazaris, Aurobindo and the Mother or Larry Wayne and Grace Johnston.

A friend described Elizabeth, despite her accomplishments, as "insecure, hyperactive, in a panic about something at all times." Her arrival at Roberts's home that night stirred one of Seth's most unforgettable conversations. Pale and tired, she was describing her natal therapy when Seth interrupted: "My dear friend, you are providing people with a framework in which you tell them that it is all right to feel the feelings that they have. You are dealing, then, with a group of beliefs. The people that come to you believe deeply that the reasons for their difficulties are beyond them, and that they cannot solve them themselves. They have been stripped of a sense of their own integrity, for they do not believe in their own power."

Seth allowed that she was using the birth sequence "in a creative manner," but he gently suggested the truth. "There is nothing 'wrong' with birth. It is a joyful, aggressive experience. People accept the idea that their problems originate from birth because it is a belief system in which you and they agree." Elizabeth used that belief system, and her clients needed it because they believed in it. "But you, for yourself and for them," Seth added, "must move also beyond it, and through it, where you realize that the idea is not valid in basic terms; that nature comes out of itself with great glory and vitality and exuberance."

Understand your "own magic," Seth urged. "Your belief works, my dear lady, because you believe in it so thoroughly. But I tell you now, there is nothing destructive in birth. When you have patients, however, who need to hang their guilt on something, and you give them birth to hang their guilt upon, then you can indeed help them, and relieve them, and provide a system for them. But you must, for yourself, feel free of the framework . . . and not be so cowed by respectable psychiatrists or psychologists who now say, 'Aha, yes, her methods work.'"

Seth urged the Truth upon her. "Now, let an old ghost tell you that I have . . . been born in more times and places than [Jane] . . . would like to admit. And let me tell you that birth is indeed an aggressive act; a joyfully aggressive act, and an intrusion into a new dimension; but it is one filled with the exhilaration of a new existence . . . The energy of my voice is nothing compared to the squalling exaltation of one child that travels from one dimension to another, and emerges victorious and yelling at the top if its lungs through the multidimensional channels of the womb!"

Seth warned if Elizabeth's patients actually believed that birth was a tragic and horrific experience they would pass it on to their children, and the idea would be "perpetuated." "You must see to it that that does not happen," he said.

He decried the dominating idea among psychiatrists and psychologists that birth was a "terrifying experience." "Now listen to me, my dear lady [Elizabeth]," he said, "for the men who threw these precepts upon you never gave birth."

Admittedly some children have great difficulty being born, but that was not the normal experience.

"Your own vitality is the only thing that gives success to your therapy," Seth exclaimed, revealing one of the great truths of healing. "You are cheating [patients] when you give them your energy . . . You must allow them to leave you behind, lovely lady, and feel instead the fantastic charge of creative energy that *was* at the birth of the universe, and *is* now, and *was* at their own birth . . . You must teach them to feel the innate wisdom and knowledge of the fetus that grew without knowing how it grew; the innate wisdom that brought them from a fetus to a fully grown adult; the innate wisdom that allowed them to grow through the nights and the days, and to emerge from a seed into the blossom of adulthood; to sense within themselves that innate wisdom and energy that was at their birth, and is now – but they have been taught to forget it.

"The birth experience is indeed an experience of power, and not of powerlessness. It is the emergence of consciousness into new, inviolate form. Only because you have been taught that a physical life is a time of trial and disaster and guilt does the framework you are using work – and it *does work.*" Seth would not deny the results of her technique. "You must rise beyond it, and become in touch with, at that moment of birth, the feeling of joyful aggression and great triumph with which the fetus so joyfully finds himself in the reality for which he was meant."

Gazing at the accolades of the psychiatric community, Seth urged her, "Be not intimidated by those who know less than you do! Do not allow them to hamper your creativity because they say you are doing well now. Do not be afraid to go beyond that point."

"Know thyself, and do yourself just honor."

Then Seth told her and all those present that the power was in that knowledge, in herself, in themselves too. "I return you then to the true infallibility, which is the infallibility of your beings; and infallibility of your strength; the infallibility of your inner knowledge," he said. "You sit before me, and your energy is unassailable; and it is indeed infallible; and it is your right. Let yourselves not be robbed of it through beliefs."

Thus he returned each to the wisdom and spontaneity of their inner selves. "You look for superior selves," he noted. "You hope for senior selves; for spirits that know what you do not know; and yet I speak for the humblest cell within your body, to whom you do not listen . . . I speak for the leaves and the wind. I speak for the knowledge that you have! I speak for the strata of your own psyches. *You* are the superior selves toward which you struggle with such great seriousness, and you cannot understand that it is precisely that seriousness that cuts you off from the intimate knowledge of the playfulness of your own being.

"When my voice is needed no longer; when you realize my voice is unnecessary; when you realize that gurus have no truths that the leaves do not possess – then will you accept and experience the spirituality of your creaturehood." Then will you know, without any telling, you are the living spirit, glory itself.

Seth ranged round the room that night speaking to those who still did not know who they were, those whose growing understanding still stood at odds with their actions. To Ira he said, "Why do you think that you must go to a guru and be whipped; or that you [George] must struggle through the worlds of art to find your being; or that you [a visitor] must come here feeling left out and alone; or that you [Elizabeth] must lead your patients to a disastrous birth encounter in order that joy be encountered; or that any of you must encounter trials before you can become enlightened?

"My purpose is to remind you of your own being; to put you in touch with what you have been taught to forget. It is, shortly, spring – and stupid flowers will be growing all over the Earth! They do not need to go to gurus or psychiatrists or priests or teachers or me to say, 'How will I manage to get one poor, puny leaf out?' Any of you have within yourselves that same joyful knowledge. I return you, then, to that vitality, to that wisdom."

Three months later, in May, Elizabeth Fehr died. Her friend in Roberts's class asked Seth why she had chosen to pass on. Said Seth, "She feared, in the framework in which she was existing, the integrity of her own being. She felt that what she was, was wrong. In her own way, she was a perfectionist, and she could not bear to be that which was wrong. Neither could she see her way out of her career beliefs.

"She'd received acclaim for ideas that she realized basically were leading her only further into a maelstrom. She felt, therefore, that it was easier, under those conditions, to leave and to begin again."

Pausing, Seth concluded, "And she is doing all right."[66]

To Knowing Within,

Anselam

The Truth Within

Dear Alma and Arn,

The importance of concepts in the mind cannot be overstated.

Misery is always concocted on rickety and ramshackle conceptions that deny your union with the Source. Each one is *Sath-chith-ananda* (Being, Awareness, Bliss), said Master Baba, and on acceptance of those truths happiness depends. "If [someone] believes that he is not *Sath*, but a lesser principle, subject to decline, decay, and death, he will be haunted by fear and uncertainty. If he thinks that he is not *Chith*, he will be caught in doubt and dialectics and will wander on the devious paths of delusion. If he assumes that he is not *Ananda*, he will be struck by every passing gust of disappointment and be subject to sorrow on every trivial defeat."[67]

So what are you now assuming about yourselves? And what do Larah and Sanson assume about themselves?

Probing,

Anselam

No Room for Sacrifice

Dear Alma and Arn,

Good thought, Alma. A *belief* is dearer to you than a *misconception*, so you are better to see yourself discarding misconceptions, mistruths, misunderstandings, which are always false. These other words have no halos.

But a caution – some of the words you use to represent false beliefs still have halos above them. Your culture has approved them, sanctified them, dressed them in the vestments of a priest. And on your own ocean you see these concepts tossed on waves nearing the shore, and you want to keep them, because they look holy, like pieces of the Cross.

As a loving mother, Alma, you want to keep sacrifice, and as a competitive father, Arn, you want to keep struggle.

The mass consciousness loves sacrifice and struggle, a rather perverse affection akin to loving grief. Likening itself to a kite, it invites the adversity of the wind to drive it higher and higher, for without resistance it does not think it can be all that it is. Difficulty stimulates genius, hardship inures the soul, it pronounces, again assuming that without these spurs the individual cannot be all that he or she is. But if you are what you are, is there only one painful, thorn-ridden way to realize it?

"At heart there are very few beings who are not enamored of struggle," said the Mother. "There are very few who would consent to having no darkness or who can conceive of light as anything other than the opposite of obscurity: 'Without shadow, there would be no painting. Without struggle, there would be no victory. Without suffering, there would be no joy.' That is what they think, and as long as they think like that, they are not yet born of the spirit."[68]

You know, life must include *shadow* so the light will appear brighter when it comes, or *sinking* so the uplift will appear grander, or *pain* so the joy will be fuller and more intense when at last it arrives. Yet you do not have to smell a stool sample to appreciate the aroma of a rose. It is as if people do not trust themselves to recognize truth without contrast, love without fear, or spirit without suffering. But the power of Spirit is not fouled with negativity or things it is not. It contains none of the refuse on Lord Dakshinamurty's ocean. It is pure light and love, and only that.

Still people will not give up struggle. They seem to require an incapacity to triumph, a debility to flourish – like a runner needing a muscle tear to win a race, or a swimmer, aquaphobia to swim, a reader, dyslexia to read, a listener, deafness to hear. There is a fundamental distortion in the mind of those who think they must *struggle* to find themselves, to be themselves. Some even reckon that the notion of search, common enough in spiritual circles, is inherently hard, scouring, exhausting. The search for truth, or for their own identity, is a struggle, they say, because *search itself* is a struggle. But "The idea of search is an error," said Baba. "Everyone already knows the truth."[69]

"People put value on having problems, difficulties, in their reality because without them they think they cannot progress, grow," says Master Wayne. "That which does not kill me makes me stronger, many believe. But these are humanistic concepts, not a spiritual ones." Many have a conception of power that requires problems to have power over. Aunts and uncles view a sickly nephew and say, "Look at that little fellow, even though he is sick, he is a fighter, struggling against that terrible allergy," and they see power as automatically involving a problem and a struggle.

Some see problems as the touchstone of the Power's effectiveness, and others see them as necessary to determine whether or not they can trust themselves. So they are always testing the trust by imposing difficulty. "Well, you managed that one," their ego says; "how about this? Now that you have mastered difficulty level one, let's go to two, then three, then four, five, six, fifty-six, a thousand and six." When the problem is in ascendancy, as it is in so many lives, you will never find that Self in which to trust. So diminished and overcast, it will be invisible to you. And all you will have left are the problems, the perplexities, the troubles, the traumas. And here you thought you needed the troubles and traumas in order to grow!

If you manufacture trouble, remember – you have an infinite ability to do so; if you then manufacture solutions, you have an infinite ability to do that too. Thus many are at war with themselves their whole lives, pitting an infinity of strife and suffering against an infinity of resolution and ease, and then repeating it over and over again. In this scenario, peace is absolutely impossible.

Some people actually value what they struggle against, but because they value it they won't let it go. "I can't give up my pain, lack, limitation, and loss," Larry hears them say. "I may need my self-pity, my poor me, my manipulation, my domination. Without struggle and sacrifice, martyrdom and misery, I would have nothing to talk about. Not only that, but I would be different if I didn't talk about them."

"There is always (it's probably inevitable) the stormy path of struggle, and then there is the sunlit path," said the Mother. "After much study and observation, I have had a sort of 'spiritual ambition' (if it can be called that) to bring to the world a sunlit path, to eliminate the necessity for struggle and suffering: something that aspires to replace this present phase of universal evolution with a less painful phase."[70]

Knowing your own worth is indispensable to this sunlit path. "If you don't know the value you are," Larry states, "you are in the pattern of self-sacrifice. Often Larry asks clients, "Where do you have value?" And they say, in their career, their service, their helping of others. Almost never do they say, *in themselves.* They value human negative need – doing things for others, never for self; doing things so the system, the parents, the clients, will approve. Human negative need always involves a focus on what you *do* instead of what you *are*, and it seeks validation from others on what you do.

I speak not of service to those in need but of doing things so others applaud. Their smile is more important than yours, as if the first causes the second. If their smile is absent, it devastates; if the confirmation is slim, it hurts. Always their fulfillment counts, not yours. They have value, you don't. Their whim and welfare matter, yours, well, only to serve theirs.

Under such circumstances, personal growth is completely aborted and personal satisfaction is fully in the hands of someone else. The result is a personality of uncompromising fragility. The very last hurdle that most people have to overcome, Grace and Larry teach, is this strangling human negative need that always places you poles from the Power and Wisdom.

"The true essence of sacrifice," said Aurobindo, "is not self-immolation, it is self-giving; its object is not self-effacement but self-fulfillment; its method is not self-mortification, but a greater life; not self-mutilation, but a transformation of our natural human parts into divine members; not self-torture, but a passage from a lesser satisfaction to a greater Ananda," a greater bliss.[71]

"In our yoga," the Mother said, "there is no room for sacrifice." To be the Power and Wisdom, say Larry and Grace, nothing is sacrificed except your misconceptions and misunderstandings.

Send comments and questions as you wish.

To Sacrifice of the Unneeded,

Anselam

Effortlessness of Spirit

Dear Arn,

Yes, struggle is second nature to your humanness; but it is alien to your Spirit which does not need struggle to create or to be. As a scholar, you are forever learning things, processing things, analyzing things, and certain that if you don't struggle and toil and grind, you will miss something or be somehow less. The Power and Wisdom, as Larry and Grace and I call it, or the Lord, as the Mother calls it, already knows everything it needs to know. It is what it is and does what it does, effortlessly.

"Oh, this tremendous labour of the mind striving to understand, toiling and giving itself headaches!" said the Mother. "It is absolutely useless, absolutely useless, no use at all, it merely increases the confusion.

"You are faced with a so-called problem; what should you say, what should you do, how should you act? There is nothing to do, nothing, you only have to say to the Lord, 'There, You see, it is like that' – that's all. And then you stay very quiet. And then quite spontaneously, without thinking about it, without reflection, without calculation, nothing, nothing, without the slightest effort – you do what has to be done. That is to say, the Lord does it, it is no longer you. He does it, He arranges the circumstances. He arranges the people, He puts the words into your mouth or your pen – He does everything, everything, everything; you have nothing more to do but to allow yourself to live blissfully.

"And it changes automatically, my child, without the slightest effort. Simply to be sincere, that is to say, to truly want everything to be right.

"But there is always something that wants to do it by itself; that's the trouble . . .

"No, you may be full of excellent goodwill and then you want to do it. That's what complicates everything. Or else you don't have faith, you believe that the Lord will not be able to do it and that you must do it yourself, because He does not know! (*Mother laughs.*) This kind of stupidity is very common.

"I am not speaking of people of no intelligence, I am speaking of people who are intelligent and who try – there is a kind of conviction, like that, somewhere, even in people who know that we live in a world of Ignorance and Falsehood and that there is a Lord who is All-Truth. They say, 'Precisely because He is All-Truth, He does not understand. (*Mother laughs.*) He does not understand our falsehood, I must deal with it myself.' That is very strong, very common."[72]

If you deal with it yourself, with just your ego, minus the power of Spirit, your efforts, Arn, will resemble the labors of Sisyphus.

The Truth is all that Spirit needs to understand, and to work its miracles effortlessly.

Love,

Anselam

Can Progress Be Too Fast?

Dear Alma and Arn,

Can you live an entire life and not grow at all spiritually, you wonder.

Imagine a frozen river in winter. Some people remain that way all their lives, frozen, inflexible, intractable, immovable, with apparently no growth, no progress. I say apparently, because even in such a state with such a life, the soul may still evolve in some way, but just how, I do not know. Perhaps there is a strengthening of its natural patience or of its natural acceptance of things and disinclination to judge, or perhaps it experiences bliss whenever the body that the Spirit inhabits simply lives, or stubbornly stands by the life it has chosen . . . I do not know.

As to your question about what seems the opposite of this kind of life – where there is so much movement, so much attempted growth, that the *speed* of spiritual progress becomes a problem – look again at the frozen river. Most people sometime in their lives are like that river. But at some point the winter ends, the sun beams with greater warmth, and impulses within demand a change, a thaw, and spring begins. Water appears on the surface and starts to flow, melting the ice beneath. The first inklings of the shift excite, the thunderous roar of the breakup exhilarates, then huge blocks of ice tumble downstream. Now, the danger arises. You see, those broken slabs of ice are really elements of your previous faith, your faith in what life held, in what you thought you were, in what you thought God was, in what you could count on, in what you had accepted consciously or unconsciously as the nature of your world. The frozen river was the structure of your very being; it supported you.

If in the rush to enlightenment you knock out all that support at once, you will destabilize yourself. You have seen wild rivers at break-up, demolishing everything in their path, dykes, docks, bridges. Each part of that demolition is an aspect of your former life – your traditions, your culture, your creeds, your concepts, much of what you had cherished, all your beliefs and everything you thought you had ever learned. That is a lot to lose overnight. A single bridge across that impassable gorge perhaps represented a core belief that life is a veil of tears lifted once or twice a decade by a well-meant kiss. But the bridge and the belief are gone now, along with their scant consolation, so what now will console you, a little voice asks. A single dyke was a cultural concept that set you apart from others, that elevated you from those who did not "understand," and now that is gone too, along with whatever sense of belonging it seemed to impart. So where now do you belong, the little voice asks.

You can see that your wish that spring become summer too soon can literally tear the footing from under you. This is why love is the greatest transforming agent, because its timing is perfect, its ministration, gentle. It begins in the right place, moves at the right pace.

Love,

Anselam

Can Progress Halt?

Dear Arn,

Notice the last word in my last letter: *pace*, the right pace.

We have been talking of desisting for sometime, but never from action, growth, or progress. You can move too quickly, true, but a far greater danger is not moving at all, or halting after a short gain. "The common herd are satisfied with pettiness and an average humanity," said Master Aurobindo.[73]

"Indeed, this is the bourgeois ideal," added the Mother, "which has deadened mankind and made man into what he is now: Work while you are young, accumulate wealth, honour, position; be provident, have a little foresight, put something by, lay up a capital, become an official – so that later when you are forty [or fifty] you 'can sit down,' enjoy your income and later your pension and, as they say, 'enjoy a well-earned rest.' To sit down, to stop on the way, not to move forward, to go to sleep, to go downhill towards the grave before one's time, cease to live the purpose of life – to sit down!

"The minute one stops going forward, one falls back. The moment one is satisfied and no longer aspires, one begins to die. Life is movement, it is effort, it is a march forward, the scaling of a mountain, the climb towards new revelations, towards future realizations. Nothing is more dangerous than wanting to rest. It is in action, in effort, in the march forward that repose must be found, the true repose of complete trust in the divine Grace.

"True repose comes from the widening, the universalization of the consciousness. Become as vast as the world and you will always be at rest."[74]

Vastness, Arn, vastness, foster it.

Anselam

Surrender

All for One and One for All

Dear Arn,

Three yeses to your latest – yes, you can reach the summits of your experience only by surrendering to the majesty of the heights; yes, the act of surrendering to your higher impulses is very simple, and yes, few do it

Surrender is the recognition, sometimes speedy, sometimes gradual, that our concepts of distance and disconnection between ourselves and the Power and Wisdom are false. There are degrees of separation where the mind is aware of its connection to the Power, or God, in some ways, but not in others, where it first understands that it sits on the surface and can go to the well and be replenished, then it senses that it is *in* the well, and finally it knows that it *is* the well.

Sai Baba put it another way – "The three stages [of enlightenment] may be described as: 'I was in the light,' 'the Light was in me,' and I am the Light.'"[1] In the first stage, one may have an awareness of the potency of the Power, the beauty of Love, the sublimity of Truth, the overcare of perfect Peace – then the feeling can lapse. In the second stage, a reminder of the Light, or the Power and Wisdom, can reanimate the feeling; and in the third stage, reminders are no longer necessary. You have become living Spirit, Spirit in action.

But surrender implies a unification of the whole being. All aspects of the self – the mental, emotional, physical, spiritual and material must be in accord, not just with the other aspects but *within* each one. For example, the mental aspect can carry conflicting beliefs: assuming perchance that the Power, or God, is both wrathful and loving (several Christian denominations convey that feeling), but the conception of wrath could prevent a surrender, equating it with capitulating to a behemoth, a monster. Or the emotional aspect, particularly in males, could grumble it has never been consulted on how it *feels* about surrendering. Or the physical aspect could wonder how the individual can participate in an endeavor that seems to deprecate the body as unnecessary and unreal.

Without a full harrowing of conflicting notions and reservations, complete consistency fails. "All the jarring elements of your nature have to be harmonized," said the Mother; "they have to be taken up one after another and unified with the central being. You may offer yourself to the [Power and Wisdom] with a spontaneous movement, but it is not possible to give yourself effectively without this unification."[2] Perhaps your knowledge, Arn, of civil wars will give some idea of the issues in unification ventures. "For your being is full of innumerable tendencies at war with one another – almost different personalities . . ." said the Mother. "When one of them gives itself to the Divine, the others come up and refuse their allegiance. 'We have not given ourselves,' they cry, and start clamouring for their independence and expression." Then you need to address each, calmly, courageously, patiently, clarifying the Truth. And when you do, the Truth has its own power. When it is said gently and to a part of you that does not know the Truth, the part usually agrees, and the falseness drops away. "Patiently you have to go round your whole being exploring each nook and corner, facing those anarchic elements in you which are waiting for their psychological moment to come up." When each part has been persuaded of the Truth, difficulties ease.

"In other words, I cannot hear you when you speak with many voices," God told his first daughter, Aala, long ago. "You have to agree with yourself, choose in unison with yourself, and speak with one voice. There cannot be a guerilla war still raging. There cannot be misgivings, reservations. The sea must be completely cleared of debris."

"I have to be all of one mind?" asked Aala.

"Yes."

To Unity Within,

Anselam

Surrender Is Not the Right Word

Dear Arn,

I don't like the term "surrender" either. The word is fouled by a military taint in our world, so one is fearful of what might happen when he capitulates, gives up hope and throws himself on the mercies of an opponent who has beaten him. This notion of surrender is particularly poignant with you, given your interest in war. You know what surrender meant in Russia after June 21, 1941.

But you are in good company.

One time Sai Baba told Dr. John Hislop, "The word 'surrender' in English is not quite correct; it is not the right word. Because when you say 'surrender,' you are separate and God is separate. That is the meaning you get. But God is not separate . . . It is not a question of surrendering . . . to some other one. *One surrenders to* HIMSELF. Recognition that the *Atma* [Spirit] is oneself is surrender . . . There is nobody who surrenders . . . There is nothing to be surrendered, nor is there anyone to accept a surrender. All is God."[3]

"'Surrender' is world language," continued Baba. "To correctly describe [it], language of the divine is needed. There is no adequate word in the English language. Therefore the use of 'surrender' goes on."[4]

Love,

Anselam

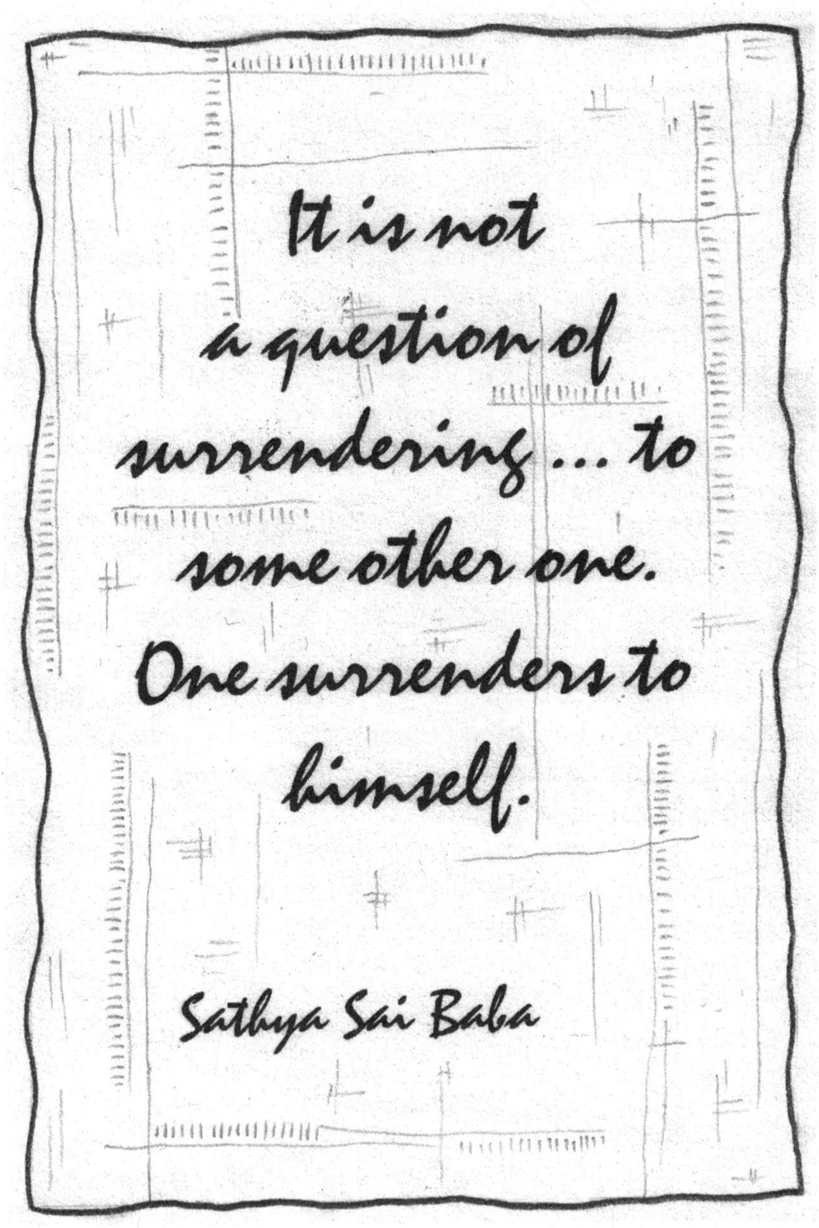
It is not
a question of
surrendering ... to
some other one.
One surrenders to
himself.
Sathya Sai Baba

Surrender Is Not Sacrifice

Dear Arn,

You have answered much of your own question. If you surrendered to yourself, surrender could hardly be called "unmanly." But you still wonder if there is something you are giving up, something you lose. You wonder if you are sacrificing your own self-made nature.

"You are leaning on your own higher self," Master Wayne says. "The last choice of the human is to become Spirit; then Spirit becomes the decision-maker."

Sacrifice is often falsely associated with this transfer of regime.

"Sacrifice," said the Mother, "is a deprivation, a self-immolation . . . a sense of forcing, a constriction, an imposed self-denial" that diminishes one's being. By sacrificing yourself in this way all the "possibilities and realizations of your personality from the most material to the highest spiritual range" are cast away. "If physically you sacrifice your life, your body, you give up all your possibilities on the material plane; you have done with the achievements of your earthly existence . . . This is an ideal that does not give room for the soul's deeper and larger spontaneities." By surrender, the Mother meant not this. "Surrender means a free total giving with all the delight of giving; there is no sense of sacrifice in it. If you have the slightest feeling that you are making a sacrifice, then it is no longer surrender." If you sense you are giving grudgingly or painfully, it is not surrender. There is a joy in true surrender, the joy of opening, deepening, expanding, the joy of shedding lack, limitation and lovelessness. "When you do anything with the sense of compression of your being, be sure you are doing it in the wrong way," the Mother said. "True surrender enlarges you, increases your capacity," provides a quality and quantity impossible for the egoic self. "You enter into a new world, into a wideness which you could not have entered if you did not surrender. It is as when a drop of water falls into the sea; if it still kept its separate identity, it would remain a little drop of water and nothing more, a little drop crushed by all the immensity around, because it has not surrendered. But, surrendering, it unites with the sea and participates in the nature and power and vastness of the whole sea."[5]

"What I am suggesting is the giving of yourself where nothing is demanded," God told Aala. "It is quite simple. If you want to be guided by the highest part of yourself, you have to hear its wisdom, and heeding it, you are actually leading yourself.

"Surrender in a spiritual sense is really giving yourself up to Love. You allow love to guide you, you allow yourself to be love. All of which is another way of saying you have finally allowed yourself to be happy. 'Sanity' would be a better name than 'surrender.' Sanity, or surrender, is finally allowing your best interests to prevail. Loving your best interests is both loving yourself and the reason why you *should* love yourself – because it is in your highest interests to do so. What will Love not give you, what will Love not protect you from?"

Aala listened quietly to her father. Then, in a hundred different places and times, she chose to be Love, which was only choosing to be what she was, or put differently, choosing to be more and more like her Father.

To Self-giving,

Anselam

One Tool

Dear Larah,

Your eye for simplicity is part of your beauty . . .

May I reply with what Master Hawkins told me?

"For significant spiritual growth, only one simple tool is required. It is merely necessary to select any simple spiritual principle that is appealing and then proceed with its application, without exception, to every area of life, both within and without. For example, one could . . . choose kindness, compassion, forgiveness, understanding, or noncritical acceptance. One could choose to be unconditionally loving or committed to seeing the innocence of life. Whatever principle is chosen then has to be applied to everyone, including oneself, without exception, and with absolute persistence. This process will bring about spiritual purification as the obstacles to these spiritual principles are brought up for examination."[6]

I was always heartened whenever Hawkins said, "Unless one was destined for enlightenment, one would not even be interested in the subject."[7]

To Destiny,

Anselam

One Approach

Dear Larah,

Tomorrow is your twentieth birthday. We have corresponded off and on for six years, and I have often shared letters to your parents with you, when appropriate and appealing. The paths I experienced in the Sea of the Self Academy I have offered, but on this important anniversary, recall Aala's gift – choice.

Nisargadatta Maharaj was conversing with his students one day about different approaches to self-realization. "Theoretically – all approaches are good," he said. "In practice, and at a given moment, you proceed by one road only. Sooner or later you are bound to discover that if you really want to find, you must dig at one place only – within."

"Surely there is something valid and valuable in every approach," suggested a student who missed the Master's meaning.

"In each case the value lies in bringing you to the need of seeking within," Maharaj elaborated. "Playing with various approaches may be due to resistance to going within, to the fear of having to abandon the illusion of being something or somebody in particular."

In my own case, Larah, I had the illusion of being an academic, one who was "comprehensive," fully aware of different approaches, different ways of seeing, and I had associated learnedness and my professional identity with this awareness. So the tendency was to sip from many cups and to demonstrate an apparent profundity in the sipping. At the same time, I sensed that my learned colleagues might wonder about my dabbling in metaphysics, dubious fare for a "regular" historian, or a "normal" scholar. In holding to this view of what I thought I was and what my colleagues expected, I was resisting the journey within myself.

"To find water, you do not dig small pits all over the place," said Maharaj, "but drill deep in one place only. Similarly, to find your self you have to explore yourself." And, you have to discard definitions you and others have imprinted on your psyche, and to overcome the resistance those definitions present to the deepest understanding of what you are. "When you realize that you are the light of the world," said the Maharaj, "you will also realize that you are the love of it."[8] But to achieve those realizations, stay with a single, proven pathway.

It is almost as if those bound for the Self in this lifetime have pre-selected their approach. Nothing else will do it, no matter how tried or true. For me, the approach taught by Larry Wayne and Grace Johnston was the main method, and somewhere in the dim past, in another life, I had agreed to teach it here. In these letters, their teachings are a single dish in the Lucullan feast of Academy renderings.

Their full plate is a separate book I am now writing.

Perhaps it is the route you will take.

Love

Anselam

The Experience of Light

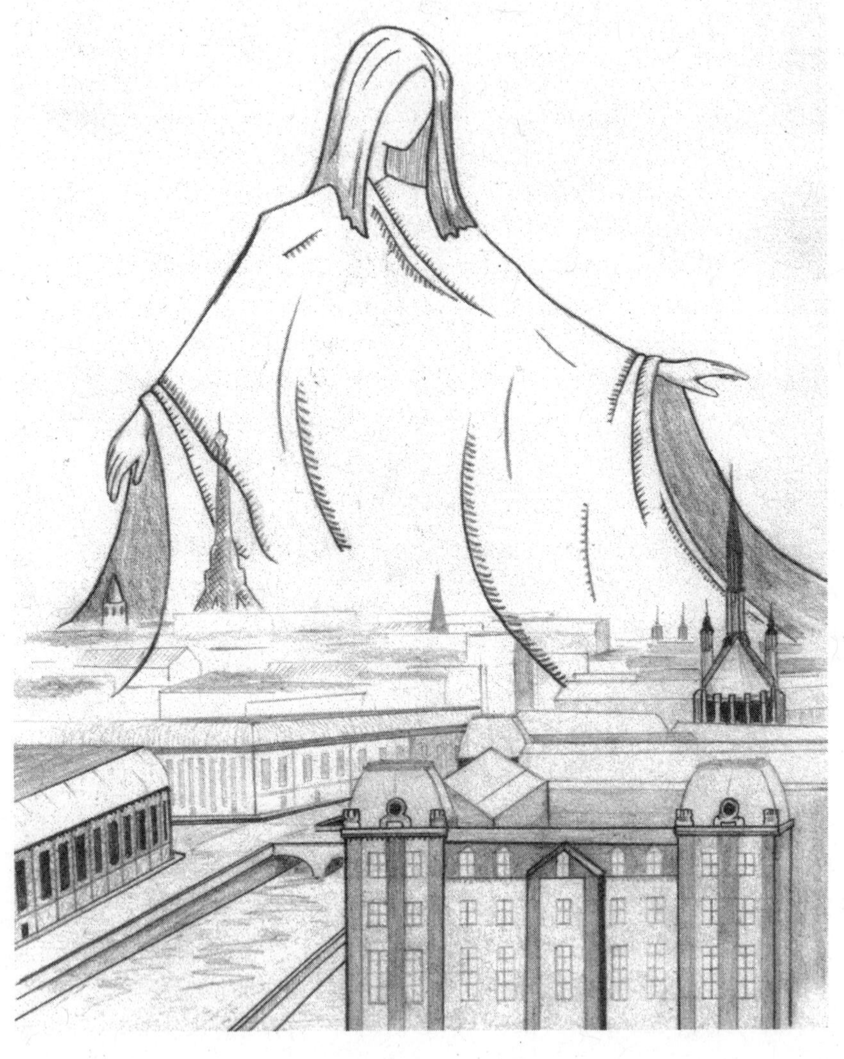

An Angel over Paris

Dear Larah,

What is possible after the surrender? One image I can never strike from my mind is of the Mother, who had merged with the Power and Wisdom early on:

"When I was a child of about thirteen, for nearly a year every night as soon as I had gone to bed it seemed to me that I went out of my body and rose straight up above the house, then above the city [of Paris] very high above. Then I used to see myself clad in a magnificent golden robe, much longer than myself; and as I rose higher, the robe would stretch, spreading out in a circle around me to form a kind of immense roof over the city. Then I would see men, women, children, old men, the sick, the unfortunate coming out from every side; they would gather under the outspread robe, begging for help, telling of their miseries, their suffering, their hardships. In reply, the robe, supple and alive, would extend towards each one of them individually, and as soon as they had touched it, they were comforted or healed, and went back into their bodies happier and stronger than they had come out of them. Nothing seemed more beautiful to me, nothing could make me happier; and all the activities of the day seemed dull and colourless and without any real life, beside this activity of the night which was the true life for me. Often while I was rising up in this way, I used to see at my left an old man, silent and still, who looked at me with kindly affection and encouraged me by his presence. This old man, dressed in a long dark purple robe, was the personification –

as I came to know later – of him who is called the Man of Sorrows.

"Now that deep experience, that almost inexpressible reality, is translated in my mind by other ideas which I may describe in this way:

"Many a time in the day and night it seems to me that I am, or rather my consciousness is, concentrated entirely in my heart which is no longer an organ, not even a feeling, but the divine Love, impersonal, eternal; and being this Love I feel myself living at the centre of each thing upon the entire earth, and at the same time I seem to stretch out immense, infinite arms and envelop with a boundless tenderness all beings, clasped, gathered, nestled on my breast that is vaster than the universe . . . Words are poor and clumsy, O divine Master, and mental transcriptions are always childish . . . But my aspiration to Thee is constant, and truly speaking, it is very often Thou and Thou alone who livest in this body, this imperfect means of manifesting Thee.

"May all beings be happy in the peace of Thy illumination!"[1]

Is this true? Did it really happen, Larah?

I think so.

To Angels,

Anselam

P.S. This captivating story I will tell to your mother, too.

One with the Soul of Cherry-Trees

Dear Larah,

You ask what will happen when you see yourself as the Power and Wisdom.

Infinity will express itself through you, but how I know not. I do know pieces of how it has expressed itself through others. In Larry and Grace there is an absolute determination, a total knowing within – as Dr. Bernadt called it – a realization that they are becoming more and more of who and what they are, that expansion is exactly what they require, that any and every obstacle will be overcome, that there is nothing more exhilarating, liberating, and ennobling than the giving of themselves to Spirit. Nothing else matters . . . It is a total dedication, a daily devotion, an intention so pure, so dynamic, that it *must* yield untold treasures.

For me, a powerful experience has been a recurrent feeling of delight, an excitement over the next discovery . . . rapturous, festive, elating, enchanting, gleeful . . .

What happens is very individual, but most often it leads to a vaster and more precious view of yourself, to an openness unparalleled, with possibilities unnumbered.

One day in April 1917, in Japan, the Mother had this vision: "A deep concentration seized upon me, and I perceived that I was identifying myself with a single cherry-blossom, then through it with all cherry-blossoms, and, as I descended deeper in the consciousness, following a stream of bluish force, I became suddenly the cherry-tree itself, stretching towards the sky, like so many arms, its innumerable branches laden with their sacrifice of flowers. Then I heard distinctly this sentence: 'Thus hast thou made thyself one with the soul of cherry-trees, and so thou canst take note that it is the Divine who makes the offering of this flower-prayer to heaven.'

"Now the blood of the cherry-tree flows in my veins, and with it flows an incomparable peace and force. What difference is there between the human body and the body of a tree? In truth, there is none: the consciousness which animates them is identically the same.

"Then the cherry-tree whispered in my ear: 'It is in the cherry-blossom that lies the remedy for the disorders of the spring.'"[2]

I first read this beautiful passage years ago, Larah, but I always wondered what the last line meant. When I was collecting the works of the Mother, one day, out of thousands of pages, I opened a single one, and here was my answer: "There are certain illnesses that people get particularly in Spring – boils, impurities of the blood, etc. – which the Japanese cure with teas made from cherry-blossoms," said the Mother. "I did not know this when I had the experience."[3]

To Cherry Blossoms,

Anselam

P.S. Larah, I was always taken by this statement of the Mother's: "Whatever be the nature, the power and the marvel of the experience, you must not be dominated by it to the point of its governing your entire being . . . When you enter in some way into contact with a force or a consciousness which is beyond yours, instead of being entirely subjugated by this consciousness or force, you must always remember that this is but one experience among thousands and thousands of others and that, consequently, it is not in any way absolute. No matter how beautiful it be, you can and you must have better ones; no matter how exceptional it be, there are others which are yet more marvelous; and however high it be, you can always climb higher in the future."[4]

I will tell this to your mother too, and you may share it with Sanson, now in grade five.

The Mother's Experience of Expansion

Dear Alma, Arn, and Larah,

"Once, for a long time, for several months, I was confined to bed and I found it rather boring – I wanted to see," related the Mother. "I was in a room and at one end there was another little room and at the end of the little room there was a kind of bridge; in the middle of the garden the bridge became a staircase leading down into a very big and very beautiful studio, standing in the middle of the garden. I wanted to go and see what was happening in the studio, for I was feeling bored in my room. So I would remain very quiet, close my eyes and send out my consciousness, little by little, little by little, little by little. And day after day – I chose a fixed time and did the exercise regularly. At first you make use of your imagination, and then it becomes a fact. After some time I really had the physical sensation that my vision was moving; I followed it and then I could see things downstairs which I knew nothing about. I would check afterwards. In the evening I would ask, 'Was this like that? And was that like this?'

"But for each one of these things you must practice for months with patience, with a kind of obstinacy. You take the senses one by one, hearing, sight, and you can even arrive at subtle realities of taste, smell and touch."[5]

Love,

Anselam

...A rosebud
is not an
imperfect rose but
is a perfect
rosebud. When
half-open, it is a
perfect unfolding
flower, and when
completely opened,
it is a perfect open
flower.

David R. Hawkins

The Perception of Perfection

Dear Alma, Arn, and Larah,

Master Hawkins described experience at the level of enlightenment:

"Action at the level 600 and above is perceived as occurring in slow motion, suspended in time and space. All is live, radiant and consciously flowing, unfolding in an exquisitely coordinate evolutionary dance in which significance and Source are overwhelming. This awesome revelation takes place without thought or conception so there is an infinite silence in the mind, which has stopped conceptualizing . . .

"Everything that exists is perfect and complete. Creation does not move from imperfection to perfection, as is witnessed by the ego, but instead moves from perfection to perfection. The illusion of moving from imperfection to perfection is a mentalization. For example, a rosebud is not an imperfect rose but is a perfect rosebud. When half-open, it is a perfect unfolding flower, and when completely opened, it is a perfect open flower. As it fades, it is a perfect faded flower, and then becomes a perfect withered plant, which then becomes perfectly dormant. Each is therefore perfect at each expansion of its expression as the emergence and unfoldment of the evolution of creation.

"Without interference by mental interpretation, the perfection of All That Exists is evidenced by its intrinsic beauty, which is the transformed physical appearance of its perfection. Without the editing and classification that emanates solely from the linear mind, everything is seen to be equally exquisite. What the world ignores as a weed is of beauty equal to that of the flower. The living-sculpture design of all nature is equal, without classification, and everything is realized to be of the same merit or worth. All is an expression of Divinity as Creation – all is equally sacred and holy."[6]

My prayer is that you will see the world that way.

You all have dived so deeply, progressed so far, that pearls of the Sea of Self are in hand, and your destiny is sure.

Love,

Anselam

The Sun's Emissaries

Dear Larah,

Here is a lovely story from Sai Baba.

"Night and light cannot co-exist," he said. "The Sun was proud that he had no enemies left. But, someone told him that he had one enemy left, viz., Darkness. Then he sent his rays, the emissaries, to seek out the foe, but wherever they went, they saw only Light, the darkness was nowhere to be found. They returned and reported. 'There was no such thing as Darkness upon the earth; we made the most rigorous search!'"[7]

This is part of turning all things to honey, part of preferring the interpretation that elevates. From the viewpoint of Light, there is no darkness, and darkness can never be. From the viewpoint of clarity, there is no confusion. From the viewpoint of purity of intention, there is no duplicity. From the viewpoint of love, there is no fear, no hate, no scorn, no cynicism . . . There is only one, only light.

Said Baba, "Love binds all hearts in a soft silken symphony. Seen through the eyes of love, all beings are beautiful, all deeds are dedicated, all thoughts are innocent, and the world is one vast kin."[8]

Larah, you are a first violin in that symphony.

Love,

Anselam

Love binds all hearts in a soft, silken symphony.
Sathya Sai Baba

Aala's Gift Again

Dear Alma and Arn and Larah,

May I recall an early letter, Alma and Arn, one you shared with Larah and Sanson?

Do you really understand the role of Aala's gift in your life – the gift of choice?

One day at the Academy in Pondicherry, the Mother told us:

"I experienced this morning, for two hours, a kind of blissful state in which there was such a clear consciousness that all the forms of life, in all the worlds and at all moments, are the expression of a choice – one chooses to be like that.

"It is very difficult to say with words . . . The kind of obligation in which one believes oneself to be living, to which one believes oneself to be submitted, had completely disappeared, and it was quite a spontaneous and natural perception that the life upon earth, and the life in other worlds, and all kinds of life upon earth and all kinds of life in other worlds are simply a question of choice: you have chosen to be like that and you choose constantly to be like this or to be like that, or whether it happens like this or it happens like that; and you choose also to believe that you are submitted to a fatality or to a necessity or to a law which compels you – everything is a question of choice. And there was a feeling of lightness, of freedom, and then a smile for everything. At the same time it gives you a tremendous power. All feeling of compulsion, of necessity – of fatality still more – had disappeared completely. All the illnesses, all the happenings, all the dramas, all that: disappeared. And this concrete and so brutal reality of the physical life: gone completely . . .

"There remains a kind of amused smile for all the complications of life – the state in which one finds oneself has been the fact of a choice, and for the individual the freedom of choice is there, and people have forgotten it."[9]

Such a revelation, admittedly, would trouble many.

But can you sense now the mood of Spirit, how the feeling of light absolutely precludes the feeling of victimhood?

To the Feeling of Light,

Anselam

Acting on the Impulse of Spirit

Dear Alma, Arn, and Larah,

Yes, follow the impulse, let Spirit act, with no hesitation, no doubt, no delay.

An example: When the philosopher George Santayana acquired a legacy, he was able to retire from the faculty at Harvard. The classroom was packed for his last word that April, and he was finishing as he noticed a forsythia beginning to bloom outside in the melting snow of Spring. He stopped suddenly, donned his cap and gloves, and stepped to the door. Turning to the class, he said quietly, "Gentlemen, I shall not be able to finish that sentence. I have just discovered that I have an appointment with April."[10]

When the supreme moment comes, you drop everything and move to the beckoning opportunity. Old ways of being, contrary habits of mind, are discarded, and the God-guided life of the Power and Wisdom, is embraced, wholly, unreservedly. It was what Christ meant when asked the price of discipleship. And when the impulse of Spirit comes, it is as if the essence deep in the Sea of Self erupts in a gargantuan geyser rushing toward the surface. The geyser, and nothing else, matters, or as Santayana said, April, and nothing else, exists.

My Eternal Love,

Anselam

P.S. Aha! A first note from young Sanson, now in grade seven, who has asked about the Academy . . . I shall answer presently. You all have laid a foundation for him in sharing the appealing stories in our correspondence.

References

I thank my colleague, Colleen Kawalilak, for reviewing the manuscript and enriching it; my son, Wesley, for his fine insight and artistry; and my friends, Larry Wayne and Grace Johnston, for their long and wise counsel.

Prolog

1. Coleman Barks, *Rumi: We Are Three* (Athens, GA: Coleman Barks, 1987), 10.

2. Sathya Sai Baba, *Sathya Sai Speaks*, Vol. 3, (Prasanthi Nilayam, India: Sri Saithya Sai Books & Publications Trust, nd), 66-67.

3. Mary Lutyens, *Krishnamurti: The Years of Fulfilment* (New York: Avon, 1983), 20.

4. Sudhakar S. Dikshit, ed., *I Am That: Talks with Sri Nisargadatta Maharaj* (Durham, NC: Acorn Press, 1996), 128-29.

5. Ibid., 202

6. Ibid., 213.

7. Tumuluru Krishna Murty, *Digest 2: Collection of Sri Sathya Sai Baba's Sayings* (Hyderabad: T. Gowri, 1994), 144.

8. Tumuluru Krishna Murty, *Digest: Collection of Sri Sathya Sai Baba's Sayings* (Milan: Sai Seva Roveredo, 1985), 271.

9. *Mother's Agenda*, 1972-1973, Vol. 13 (New York: Institute of Evolutionary Research, 1983), 41.

10. Dikshit, *I Am That*, 216.

11. Kriyananda, (J. Donald Walters), compiler, *The Essence of Self-Realization: The Wisdom of Paramhansa Yogananda* (Nevada City, CA: Crystal Clarity Publishers, 1990), 155.

Teachers

1. Kriyananda (J. Donald Walters), compiler, *The Essence of Self-Realization: The Wisdom of Paramahansa Yogananda* (Nevada City, CA: Crystal Clarity Publishers, 1991), 123-125.

2. Sudhakar S. Dikshit, ed., *I Am That: Talks with Sri Nisargadatta Maharaj* (Durham, N.C., Acorn Press, 1996), 274

3. C.M. Sahni and Robert McClung, eds., *Gems of Wisdom: Quotations from Bhagawan Sri Sathya Sai Baba* (Prasanthi Nilayam: Sri Sathya Sai Books & Publications Trust, nd), 390

4. The Mother, *Words of the Mother*, 2 (Pondicherry, Sri Aurobindo Ashram Trust, 2004), 60.

5. Tumuluru Krishna Murty, *Digest 2: Collection of Sri Sathya Sai Baba's Sayings* (Prasanthi Nilayam, India: Sri Sathya Sai Books & Publications Trust, 1994), 24-25.

6. Clifton Fadiman, ed., *The Little, Brown Book of Anecdotes* (Boston: Little Brown, 1985), 400.

7. Peter Hees, *Sri Aurobindo: A Brief Biography* (Oxford, Oxford University Press, 1997), 12.

8. Ibid., 56.

9. Ibid., 94.

10. Sri Aurobindo, *Sri Aurobindo on Himself and the Mother* (Pondicherry, Sri Aurobindo Ashram, 1953), 434.

11. Ibid., 150.

12. Sri Aurobindo, *On Himself*, Sri Aurobindo Birth Centenary Library, Vol. 26 (Pondicherry, Sri Aurobindo Ashram Trust, 1972), 346.

13. Sri Aurobindo, *The Harmony of Virtue,* Sri Aurobindo Birth Centenary Library, Vol. 3 (Pondicherry, Sri Aurobindo Ashram Trust, 1972), 430.

14. Sri Aurobindo, *The Future Poetry*, Sri Aurobindo Birth Centenary Library, Vol. 9 (Pondicherry, Sri Aurobindo Ashram Trust, 1972), 284.

15. Ibid., 229.

16. David Godman, "Remembering Nisargadatta Maharaj," http://davidgodman.org/interviews/nis2.shtml

17. Ibid.

18. Ibid.

19. David Godman, "Remembering Nisargadatta Maharaj," http://davidgodman.org/interviews/nis3.shtml

Being

1. Paramahansa Yogananda, *The Collected Talks and Essays*, Vol. 3 *Journey to Self-Realization: Discovering the Gifts of the Soul* (Los Angeles: Self Realization Fellowship, 1997), 25-27.

2. Paramahansa Yogananda, *Where There Is Light* (Los Angeles: Self-Realization Fellowship, 1989), 25.

3. *A Course in Miracles*, Text, (New York, Viking: 1996), 76.

4. Ibid., Workbook, 220.

5. Patricia Lorenz, "The Golden Crane," in Jack Canfield and Mark Victor Hansen, *A 3rd Serving of Chicken Soup for the Soul* (Deerfield Beach, FL: Health Communications, 1996), 140-42.

6. *A Course in Miracles*, Text, 103-104.

7. Ibid.

8. Sathya Sai Baba, *Sathya Sai Speaks,* Vol. 3 (Prasanthi Nilayam, India: Sri Sathya Sai Books & Publications Trust, nd), 66.

9. David C. Jones, *Sayings for Sufferers* (Calgary: Detselig, 1998), 50.

10. The Mother, *On Thoughts and Aphorisms: Collected Works of the Mother,* Vol. 10 (Pondicherry: Sri Aurobindo Ashram Trust, 1977), 164-65.

11. Anthony De Mello, *The Song of the Bird* (New York: Doubleday/Image Books, 1984), 20.

12. Sathya Sai Baba, *Sathya Sai Speaks*, Vol. 10 (Prasanthi Nilayam, India: Sri Sathya Sai Books & Publications Trust, nd), 74.

13. Ibid., 30.

14. David R. Hawkins, *The Eye of the I From Which Nothing Is Hidden* (West Sedona, AZ: Veritas Publications, 2001), 36.

15. David C. Jones, ed., *Sayings of Sathya Sai Baba* (Calgary: Detselig, 2008), 96.

16. Sathya Sai Baba, *Sathya Sai Speaks,* Vol. 5 (Prasanthi Nilayam, India: Sri Sathya Sai Books & Publications Trust, nd), 167-69.

17. Sudhakar S. Dikshit, ed., *I Am That: Talks with Sri Nisargadatta Maharaj* (Durham, NC: Acorn Press, 1996), 149, emphasis mine.

18. Clifton Fadiman, ed., *The Little, Brown Book of Anecdotes* (Boston: Little Brown, 1985), 449.

19. Tony Augarde, ed., *The Oxford Dictionary of Modern Quotations* (Oxford: Oxford University Press, 1991), 55.

20. Dikshit, *I Am That*, 125.

21. Ibid., 145.

22. The Mother, *On Thoughts and Aphorisms*, 303-304.

23. Ibid.

24. Fadiman, *Anecdotes*, 248.

25. Ibid., 248.

26. Ibid., 249.

27. Ibid., 248.

28. Ibid., 122-23.

29. Ibid., 382-83.

30. David Niven, from *The Moon's a Balloon*, in Max Hastings, ed., *The Oxford Book of Military Quotations* (Oxford, NY: Oxford University Press, 1985), 468-69.

31. Mary Lutyens, *Krishnamurti: The Years of Fulfillment* (New York: Avon, 1983), 197.

32. Ibid., 33.

33. Ibid., 20.

34. Pupul Jayakar, *Krishnamurti: A Biography* (San Francisco: Harper and Row, 1986), 62.

35. Ibid., 197-198.

36. Erlandur Haraldsson, *Modern Miracles: An Investigative Report on Psychic Phenomena Associated with Sathya Sai Baba* (Mamaroneck, NY: Hastings House, 1987), 85

37. John S. Hislop, *Conversations with Bhagavan Sri Sathya Sai Baba* (Prasanthi Nilayam, India: Sri Sathya Sai Books & Publications Trust, 1985c), 150.

38. Sharon Salzberg, *Lovingkindness: The Revolutionary Art of Happiness* (Boston: Shambala, 1995), 13-14, 112-113.

39. Hislop, *Conversations*, 13.

40. Tumuluru Krishna Murty, compiler, *Sai Avatar*, Vol. 2 (Calcutta: C.J. Gandhi Welfare Trust, nd), 175

41. C.M. Sahni & Robert McClung, et. al., *Gems of Wisdom* (Puttaparthi, India: Sri Sathya Sai Books & Publications Trust, nd.), 66

42. Hislop, *Conversations*, 116-17.

43. The Mother, *Words of the Mother,* 2 (Pondicherry: Sri Aurobindo Ashram Trust, 2004), 294, Mother's emphasis.

44. Ibid., 122.

45. Larry Wayne and Grace Johnston, *The Eleven Keys to Miraculous Success!* (2007), 61

46. Jones, *Sayings of Sathya Sai Baba*, 92.

47. Larry Dossey, *Reinventing Medicine: Beyond Mind-Body to a New Era of Healing* (New York: HarperCollins, 1999), 62.

48. Ibid., 42.

49. Ibid., 69-70.

50. Hislop, *Conversations*, 37-39; Sathya Sai Baba, *Sathya Sai Speaks*, Vol. 11 (Prashanti Nilayam, India: Sri Sathya Sai Books & Publications Trust, nd), 41.

51. *A Course in Miracles*, Workbook, 217.

52. *The URANTIA Book* (Chicago: URANTIA Foundation, 1981), 1898.

53. "Amish mourn school shooter," *Calgary Herald*, October 8, 2006, A5.

54. The Mother, *On Thoughts and Aphorisms*, 47.

55. Brant House, ed., *Lincoln's Wit* (New York: Ace Books, 1958), 195.

56. Sathya Sai Baba, *Sathya Sai Speaks,* Vol. 2 (Prashanti Nilayam, India: Sri Sathya Sai Books & Publications Trust, nd), 249.

57. The Best of Bits and Pieces, "Good News," *A 3rd Portion of Chicken Soup for the Soul* (Deerfield Beach, FL: Health Communications, 1996), 237.

58. Anthony De Mello, *One Minute Wisdom* (New York: Doubleday/Image Books, 1988), 133.

59. Baba, *Sathya Sai Speaks*, Vol. 3, 100-101.

60. Baba, *Sathya Sai Speaks*, Vol. 11, 164.

61. Fadiman, *Anecdotes*, 553.

62. The approach of Masters Wayne and Johnston is collated in three books: *Awaken the God or Goddess within You, 11 Keys to Miraculous Success!*, and *Living in Power and Wisdom: The Secret to Re-Creating Yourself and Your World*. The book of Wayne and Johnston and their teachings I am presently writing.

63. Dikshit, *I Am That*, 121.

64. *A Course in Miracles*, Workbook, 393.

65. Ibid., 402.

66. Ibid., 403.

67. De Mello, *One Minute Wisdom*, 199.

68. Baba, *Sathya Sai Speaks*, Vol. 3, 244.

69. Baba, *Sathya Sai Speaks*, Vol. 2, 8-9. My emphasis.

70. Jones, *Sayings of Sathya Sai Baba*, 46.

Desisting

1. Sathya Sai Baba, *Sathya Sai Speaks,* Vol. 9 (Prasanthi Nilayam, India: Sri Sathya Sai Books & Publications Trust, nd), 77.

2. Sudhakar S. Dikshit, ed., *I Am That: Talks with Sri Nisargadatta Maharaj* (Durham, NC: Acorn Press, 1996), 89-90.

3. Clifton Fadiman, ed., *The Little, Brown Book of Anecdotes* (Boston: Little Brown, 1985), 537-538.

4. Idries Shah, *The Sufis* (Garden City, New York: Anchor Books, 1971), 67.

5. Paramahansa Yogananda, *Autobiography of a Yogi* (Los Angeles: Self Realization Fellowship, 1971), 122.

6. M.P. Pandit, ed., *Gems from Aurobindo,* 3rd series (Twin Lakes, WI: Lotus Light Publication, 1995), 98.

7. Mary Lutyens, *Krishnamurti: The Years of Fulfilment* (New York: Avon, 1983), 197-198.

8. Rabindranath Tagore, *Fireflies* (New York: Macmillan, 1946), 22.

9. Rabindranath Tagore, "Stray Birds," in *Collected Poems and Plays of Rabindranath Tagore* (London: Macmillan, 1967), 317.

10. Ibid., 291.

11. Fulton Oursler, quoted in David C. Jones, ed., *Sayings for Sufferers* (Calgary: Detselig, 1998), 24.

12. Anthony De Mello, *One Minute Wisdom* (New York: Doubleday/Image Books, 1988), 87.

13. Sathya Sai Baba, *Sathya Sai Speaks,* Vol. 4 (Prasanthi Nilayam, India: Sri Sathya Sai Books & Publications Trust, nd), 141.

14. Sri Aurobindo, *Thoughts and Aphorisms* (Pondicherry: Sri Aurobindo Ashram Trust, 1982), 91.

15. Sathya Sai Baba, *Sathya Sai Speaks,* Vol. 3 (Prasanthi Nilayam, India: Sri Sathya Sai Books & Publications Trust, nd), 27-28.

16. Yogananda, *Autobiography*, 133.

17. Ibid.

18. Ibid., 134-35.

19. Baba, *Sathya Sai Speaks,* Vol. 3, 174, 237-38.

20. Ibid., 183-84,

21. N. Kasturi, *Sathyam Sivam Sundarum, Part lV, The Life of Bhagavan Sri Sathya Sai Baba* (Prasanthi Nilayam, India: Sri Sathya Sai Books & Publications Trust, nd), 163-67.

22. Swami Kriyananda (J.Donald Walters), *The Path: Autobiography of a Western Yogi* (Nevada City, CA: Ananda Publications, 1979), 335-36.

23. Michael Talbot, *The Holographic Universe* (New York: Harper Perennial, 1991), 102.

24. The Mother, *On Thoughts and Aphorisms: Collected Works of the Mother, Centenary Edition*, Vol. 10 (Pondicherry: Sri Aurobindo Ashram Trust, 1977), 77-78.

25. Sathya Sai Baba, *Sathya Sai Speaks*, Vol. 14 (Prashanti Nilayam, India: Sri Sathya Sai Books & Publications Trust, nd), 32.

26. David R. Hawkins, *The Eye of the I From Which Nothing Is Hidden* (West Sedona, AZ: Veritas Publishing, 2001), 67.

27. Paramahansa Yogananda, *God Talks with Arjuna: The Bhagavad Gita - Royal Science of God-Realization* (Los Angeles: Self-Realization Fellowship, 1995), 7.

28. David R. Hawkins, *Truth vs Falsehood: How to Tell the Difference* (Toronto: Axial Publishing, 2005), 323.

29. Ibid., 245.

30. Ibid., 291.

31. David R. Hawkins, *Transcending the Levels of Consciousness: The Stairway to Enlightenment* (West Sedona, AZ: Veritas Publishing, 2006), 325.

32. Aurobindo, *On Himself*, Sri Aurobindo Centenary Library, Vol. 26 (Pondicherry: Sri Aurobindo Ashram Trust, 1972), 76.

33. M.P. Pandit, compiler, *Gems from Sri Aurobindo*, 1st Series (Wilmot, WI: Lotus Light Publications, 1991), 13.

34. The Mother, *On Thoughts and Aphorisms*, 348.

35. Ibid., 283.

36. Ibid.

37. "A Hero of Our Time," http://otaku.memory-motel.net/stauffenberg/ And "Count Claus von Stauffenberg," http://www.moreorless.au.com/heroes/stauffenberg.html

38. The Mother, *On Thoughts and Aphorisms*, 285.

39. Ibid.

40. Ibid., 67-68.

41. Ibid., 157.

42. Robert G. Ingersoll, *The Works of Robert G. Ingersoll.* Vol. 1 (New York: Dresden Publishing Co., 1902), 220-222.

43. *A Course in Miracles* (New York: Viking, 1996), 173.

44. The Mother, *On Thoughts and Aphorisms*, 122.

45. H.L. Mencken, quoted in David C. Jones, ed., *Sayings for Cynics* (Calgary: Detselig, 1999), 63.

46. The Mother, *On Thoughts and Aphorisms*, 259.

47. "Germans love David Hasselhoff, mock old rockers," *Calgary Herald*, August 28, 2007, C5.

48. De Mello, *One Minute Wisdom*, 16.

49. Fadiman, *Anecdotes*, 402.

50. Ibid., 388.

51. David R. Hawkins, *Reality, Spirituality and Modern Man* (Toronto: Axial Publishing Company, 2008), 35.

52. Hawkins, *Transcending*, 249.

53. Larry Dossey, *Reinventing Medicine: Beyond Mind-Body to a New Era of Healing* (New York: HarperCollins, 1999), 89, quoting Russell from *Second Wind*, 1979.

54. Fadiman, *Anecdotes*, 171.

55. Hawkins, *Truth vs Falsehood*, 237-39.

56. These and Hawkins other books, including, *The Eye of the I From Which Nothing Is Hidden* (2001) and *Reality and Subjectivity* (2003), I highly recommend.

57. David R. Hawkins, *Power vs. Force: The Hidden Determinants of Human Behavior* (Carlsbad, CA: Hay House, 1995), 16-17.

58. David C. Jones, *Meditations of Anselam: Letters from an Elder Teacher* (Calgary: Detselig, 2005), 31-39.

59. Edmund Fuller, ed., *2500 Anecdotes for All Occasions* (New York: Avenel Books, 1978), 58-59.

60. My thanks to Jeff Gilbert for these examples of disturbed prose.

61. Fuller, *2500 Anecdotes*, 16.

62. *Mother's Agenda, 1964,* Vol. 5 (New York: Institute for Evolutionary Research, 1988), 23.

63. N. Sri Ram, *Thoughts for Aspirants* (Wheaton, IL: Theosophical Publishing House, 1989), 16-21.

64. Herbert Benson with Marg Stark, *Timeless Healing: The Power and Biology of Belief* (New York: Scribner, 1996), 40-41.

65. Talbot, *The Holographic Universe*, 93-94.

66. Susan B. Watkins, *Conversations with Seth: The Story of Jane Roberts's ESP Class,* Vol. 2 (New York: Prentice Hall, 1986), 596-606.

67. Baba, *Sathya Sai Speaks*, Vol. 14, 19.

68. *Mother's Agenda, 1951-1960,* Vol. 1 (Paris: Foundation for Evolutionary Research, 1970), 247.

69. John S Hislop, *Conversations with Bhagavan Sri Sathya Sai Baba* (Prasanthi Nilayam, India: Sri Sathya Sai Books and Publications Trust, 1985c), 90.

70. *Mother's Agenda, 1961,* Vol. 2 (Paris: Institutes de Recherches Evolutives, 1981), 336.

71. Sri Aurobindo, *The Synthesis of Yoga, Parts One and Two,* Sri Aurobindo Birth Centenary Library-De Luxe Edition (Pondicherry: Sri Aurobindo Ashram Trust, 1970), 101.

72. The Mother, *On Thoughts and Aphorisms,* 152-54.

73. The Mother, *Questions and Answers 1957-58, Collected Works of the Mother,* Vol. 9 (Pondicherry: Sri Aurobindo Ashram Trust, 1977), 64.

74. Ibid, 65.

Surrender

1. Sathya Sai Baba, *Sathya Sai Speaks*, Vol. 10 (Prasanthi Nilayam, India: Sri Sathya Sai Books & Publications Trust, nd), 231.

2. The Mother, *Questions and Answers, Collected Works of the Mother,* Vol. 3 (Pondicherry: Sri Aurobindo Ashram Press, 1977), p. 126.

3. John S. Hislop, *Conversations with Bhagavan Sri Sathya Sai Baba* (Prasanthi Nilayam, India: Sri Sathya Sai Books and Publications Trust, 1985c), 122, italics mine.

4. Ibid., 123.

5. The Mother, *Questions and Answers,* 114-115.

6. David R. Hawkins, *The Eye of the I From Which Nothing is Hidden* (West Sedona, AZ: Veritas Publications, 2001), 224.

7. Ibid., p. 36.

8. Sudhakar S. Diksit, ed., *I Am That: Talks with Sri Nisargadatta Maharaj* (Durham, NC: The Acorn Press, 1996), 202.

The Experience of Light

1. The Mother, *Prayers and Meditations, Collected Works of the Mother,* Vol. 1 (Pondicherry, Sri Aurobindo Ashram Press: 1979), 81-82.

2. Ibid., 359.

3. The Mother, *More Answers from the Mother, Collected Works of the Mother,* Vol. 17 (Pondicherry: Sri Aurobindo Ashram Press, 1987), 186.

4. Satprem, *Sri Aurobindo or the Adventure of Consciousness* (New York: Harper & Row, 1968), 158.

5. The Mother, *On Thoughts and Aphorisms: Collected Works of the Mother,* Vol. 10 (Pondicherry: Sri Aurobindo Ashram Trust, 1977), 134.

6. David R. Hawkins, *Transcending the Levels of Consciousness: The Stairway to Enlightenment* (West Sedona, AZ: Veritas Publishing, 2006), 275-78.

7. Sathya Sai Baba, *Sathya Sai Speaks,* Vol. 3 (Prasanthi Nilayam, India: Sri Sathya Sai Books & Publications Trust, nd), 198.

8. Tumuluru Krishna Murty, ed., *Digest: Collection of Sri Sathya Sai Baba's Sayings* (Hyderabad, India: T. Gowri, 1994), 192-93.

9. The Mother, *Notes on the Way: Collected Works of the Mother,* Vol. 11 (Pondicherry: Sri Aurobindo Asharam Trust, 1980), 30.

10. Clifton Fadiman, ed., *The Little, Brown Book of Anecdotes* (Boston: Little Brown, 1985), 487.